AROUND THE WORLD IN 80 DAYS
THE 1874 PLAY

Publications of the North American Jules Verne Society

The Palik Series (edited by Brian Taves)

The Marriage of a Marquis
   Contributors: Edward Baxter, Jean-Michel Margot, Walter James Miller, Kieran M. O'Driscoll, Brian Taves

   Shipwrecked Family: Marooned with Uncle Robinson
      Translated by Sidney Kravitz; Introduction by Brian Taves

      Mr. Chimp, and Other Plays
      Translated by Frank Morlock; Introduction by Jean-Michel Margot

      The Count of Chanteleine: A Tale of the French Revolution
      Translated by Edward Baxter; Introduction by Brian Taves;
      Notes by Garmt de Vries-Uiterweerd, Volker Dehs

      Vice, Redemption, and the Distant Colony: Stories by Jules Verne and Michel Verne
      Translated, with notes, by Kieran M. O'Driscoll

      Bandits & Rebels
      Translated by Edward Baxter; Introduction by Daniel Compère

      Golden Danube
      Translated, with notes, by Kieran M. O'Driscoll

      (Other volumes in preparation)

Editorial Committee of the North American Jules Verne Society:

   Henry G. Franke III   Dr. Terry Harpold
   Jean-Michel Margot   Dr. Brian Taves

AROUND THE WORLD IN 80 DAYS
THE 1874 PLAY

by Jules Verne and Adolphe d'Ennery

Illustrated with the Engravings from the Original French Publication

Contributors: Philippe Burgaud, Jean-Louis Trudel, Jean-Michel Margot, Brian Taves

Edited by Brian Taves for the North American Jules Verne Society

The Palik Series

BearManor Fiction
2012

Around the World in 80 Days – The 1874 Play
by Jules Verne and Adolphe d'Ennery

© 2012 by the North American Jules Verne Society

All rights reserved.

For information, address:

BearManor Fiction
P. O. Box 71426
Albany, GA 31708

bearmanormedia.com

North American Jules Verne Society: najvs.org

Typesetting and layout by John Teehan

Cover design from an original 19th century French edition

Published in the USA by BearManor Media

ISBN—1-59393-384-3
978-1-59393-384-5

Table of Contents

Introduction 1
   by Philippe Burgaud,
   with Jean-Michel Margot and Brian Taves

Around the World in 80 Days – The 1874 Play 33
   by Jules Verne and Adolphe d'Ennery

Afterword: The Meridians and the Calendar 151
   by Jules Verne
   Translated and Annotated by Jean-Louis Trudel

Appendix: The Play on Screen 157
   by Brian Taves

Illustrations 167

Acknowledgements 169

Contributors 171

The Palik Series 173

*For Robert Pourvoyeur
who over four decades sought to
promote understanding of Verne's career
as a playwright*

INTRODUCTION

by Philippe Burgaud
with Jean-Michel Margot and Brian Taves

This is the second volume devoted to Verne and theater in the North American Jules Verne Society's Palik Series, because his output for the stage almost rivals his novels in importance. Verne not only achieved his first notice as a playwright, but adapted some of his novels to the stage. His most famous book actually began as an unproduced play, was rewritten as an acclaimed novel, and in a wholly new stage version, became a hit play. The original translation forms the core of this volume, a faithful version of the original playscript commissioned at the time of the purchase of American theatrical rights. This was undertaken by the Kiralfy brothers, theatrical impresarios who led in offering Verne's own plays to audiences in the United States during the last three decades of the 19th century. The following pages explore first the genesis and reception of the play, then how it was brought to the United States.

A Literary and a Stage Hit

Although generally thought of as a writer of science fiction, half of Verne's output belonged to another genre, adventure stories, and *Around the World in Eighty Days* is the best-remembered example. Adventure emerged as a generic tradition during the 19th century, and a key element of such fiction was its celebration of the opening of distant lands to European exploration and colonization. Verne's adventure stories usually concern a journey and survival, combining travel, geography, political commentary, a touch of mystery, and sometimes even comedy. These elements are particularly notable not only in *Around the World in Eighty Days*, but also *Les Tribulations d'un Chinois en Chine* (*The Tribulations of a Chinese in China*, 1879), *L'École des Robinsons* (*The School for Robinsons*, 1882), *Kéraban-le-têtu* (*Keraban the Inflexible*, 1883), *Clovis Dardentor* (1896), and *Le Testament d'un excentrique* (*The Will of an Eccentric*, 1899). The contest that executed *The Will of an Eccentric* was a domestic version of *Around the World in Eighty Days*, with a cast of uniquely American characters to rival those encountered by Phileas Fogg.

Verne's talent as a humorist has been unjustly overlooked, and was highlighted in the first volume of the Palik series, *The Marriage of a Marquis*. Vernian humor often finds its basis in bizarre characters, many of them placed in unusual locales, such as Kin-Fo in China, Keraban in Turkey, or Phileas Fogg in virtually any corner of the world. Satire was a prominent element, whether of evolution in "Le Humbug" ("The Humbug," 1910) and *Aventures de la famille Raton* (*Adventures of the Rat Family*, 1891), or the parable of survival on a desert island, *The School for Robinsons*. In *Une Fantaisie du Docteur Ox* (*A Fancy of Doctor Ox*, 1872), Verne cleverly mocks his own literary formula, with the mad escapade of a scientist who fills a small town's atmosphere with oxygen, speeding up the pace of living to a frenzy.

Around the World in Eighty Days, on one level a travel adventure, is also a satire, a rebuke to British insularity and imperialism, on whose global empire, in this story, the sun truly never sets. Phileas Fogg's journey, ostensibly initiated as a wager, is equally an unconscious flight from the minimal human contact he has at the whist table of the typically British Reform Club. Fogg begins with contempt for everyone who is not English, from Americans to Asians, seeing them all as equally barbaric and foreign. The journey provides the opposite of his expectation: Fogg's anticipated, well-timed and perfectly scheduled itinerary runs steadily more afoul of chance and circumstance, as the mechanics of his means of travel break down completely. By encountering numerous foreign cultures, Phileas Fogg's unflappability is steadily shaken until his English reserve and manners are undermined. His growing camaraderie with Passepartout, and eventual marriage to the Indian woman, Aouda, highly unusual in the late 19th century, are a rejection of the proud tradition of the British aristocracy. The actual winning of the wager becomes a pure accident predicated on Fogg's apparent loss and marriage to Aouda.

Introduction | 3

Two examples from a series of sixteen postcards from the play, issued around 1900.

1880 caricature of the famous novelist and playwright.

The origin of *Le Tour du monde en quatre-vingts jours* (*Around the World in Eighty Days*) was only recently discovered. The story was first developed in 1872 as a play. Though the concept was Verne's, a first draft was written in collaboration with Edouard Cadol (1831-1898).[1] Cadol was a playwright of the "Comédie française," and the initial Verne-Cadol effort had four acts and sixteen tableaux (separate stage pictures providing background for the scenes). However, when this draft was rejected by several theater directors, Cadol, always difficult to work with, became angry and impatient. He left the project, and without his input, Verne wrote the novel, *Around the World in Eighty Days*, which was serialized during the last quarter of 1872 in *Le Temps*, a large Parisian newspaper. Even at that point it won global notice, and upon publication as a book in 1873, quickly became a bestseller.[2]

The Théâtre de la Porte Saint-Martin, after renovations, reopened September 27, 1873, and its directors, Eugène Ritt (1817-1898) and Henri Larochelle (1827-1884), who had rejected the Verne-Cadol draft, became interested in a new theatrical adaptation taken from the novel. Ritt and Larochelle were about to mount *Les Deux orphelines*, by the prolific playwright Adolphe Philippe (1811-1899), known as Adolphe d'Ennery (also written Dennery). D'Ennery was a specialist in the "pieces à grand spectacle" (plays with great spectacle), and Ritt and Larochelle suggested that Verne and d'Ennery meet. D'Ennery, in an 1896 letter to the newspaper *Le Figaro*, related how this first meeting took place.

> Jules Verne came one day to see me, sent by the directors of the Porte Saint Martin to propose to write with him a drama based on his novel and the following dialogue was established between us:
> As far as I know, the play is completely finished.
> No, it's only at the beginning.
> Do you have a collaborator, Ed Cadol?
> We are not collaborating anymore.
> What happens with his share of work?

---

1. Volker Dehs, "La polémique Verne-Cadol," *Bulletin de la Société Jules Verne*, No. 120 (1996), 55.

2. Verne scholars refer to the novel as *Around the World in Eighty Days* and to the play as *Around the World in 80 Days*.

> M. Ritt opposes formally that it is communicated to you.
> Why?
> He disagrees with our beginning, and fears that you would follow the path we took.[3]

D'Ennery agreed to take on the play and Verne was very pleased with the collaboration. He made frequent trips to d'Ennery's house in Antibes, "The Green Oaks," to labor with him, and to become more knowledgeable about the art of theatrical writing. In November 1873, Verne wrote to his publisher, Pierre-Jules Hetzel, who often wintered in Menton, in the south of France. "My dear Hetzel, I am for eight days in your winter country, spending time in this beautiful property you know outside… I am extremely well received here and working hard. I'm learning things I didn't know. It's no more a simple cutting of the book in pieces, it's a real play, and I think that will be very interesting and diverse."[4] The collaboration took several months; Verne was in Antibes in December 1873 and again in February, March and April, 1874.

Meanwhile, a controversy between Verne and Cadol developed in the newspapers. Cadol published letters claiming authorship of the play and the novel. Jules Verne replied, and the relationship between the two men deteriorated. To have a free hand with d'Ennery, Verne accepted a financial compromise, Cadol receiving 25% of the profits of the play, Verne another 25%, and d'Ennery 50%.

The premiere of the play took place Saturday, November 7, 1874 at the Théâtre de la Porte Saint Martin, and Verne was among the spectators. Initially, the play was structured in five acts, one prologue, and fifteen scenes. Given the many changes asked by the directors during the summer of 1874, the spectators soon enjoyed a great show in five acts and twenty-two tableaux, combined with many ballets. The different stages of the world tour offered a perfect opportunity to multiply picturesque sets and enchanting figures in national costumes, exotic dances and ballets, merged with dramatic theatrical sequences.

---

3. Dehs, 17.

4. Letter n° 183, *Correspondance inédite de J. Verne et P-J Hetzel*, Volume I (Geneva: Slatkine, 1999), 219.

Edouard Cadol.

Théâtre de la Porte St. Martin.

The Paris press was full of praise for this new kind of theater, and all the major newspapers published reviews speaking highly of the quality of the show. Many articles had engravings showing the most picturesque scenes. *L'Illustration, Journal Universel*, in an unsigned review, described it as a "fairy play."[5] Another example was printed by *Le Monde illustré*.

> The Porte Saint Martin shows a great success with a play that involves both drama and magic… This dramatic adaptation of a popular book has been very appreciated… The staging is not only gorgeous, which is essential, but it's also very intelligently done. Nothing was missing: the steamer at full steam, the railways at full speed, we cross seas, we walk through forests, we climb mountains. We get shiny glimpses of famous cities, and specimens of various human races.[6]

In a third review, for *L'Univers Illustré*, the journalist Gérome summarized the plot of the play and its differences from the novel, on two entire columns.

> But you could tell me, we know this amazing journey, most of these wondrous adventures are not new for us and all of the characters, except Archibald Corsican, Misses Margaret and Nemea, are old friends. Yes, you're right, without doubt, if you have read this delightful book called *Around the World in Eighty Days*. But take travel, adventures, characters, out of the book and carry it on stage. Ask the Théâtre de la Porte Saint Martin to give you its decorators to paint the Bay of Suez, the Indian burial ground, the sun-drenched landscapes of the Far East, the snow and icy torrents of the Rocky Mountains, the swells of the ocean, its designers to give their true costumes to Arabs, Indians, Malays, Indians of the Far West, and its ballet masters to embellish entertainment… You

---

5. *L'Illustration, Journal Universel* (November 14, 1874), 315.
6. Charles Monselet, *Le Monde Illustré* (November 14, 1874), 315.

will get this fairy play I just mentioned, without fairies. To achieve it, it needs the original spirit of Jules Verne, the invention and experience of Mr. d'Ennery and the magnificence of one of the most beautiful theaters in Paris, which does not even hesitate before the luxury of a live elephant.[7]

Indeed, as these reviews suggested, the plot of the novel had to be modified to add episodes with a more theatrical flavor as well as to provide new elements for audiences who had already read the book. Verne and d'Ennery downplayed the centrality of Fogg and his journey in favour of new characters and situations. Fogg became less insular, apparently more accustomed to travel, keeping a bag always packed just in case.

As the member of a club of eccentrics in London, rather than the withdrawn, conservative Reform Club, Fogg became less of a unique character. Among the eccentrics, Fogg seems more conventional, and is the easiest man to serve; to secure him as his master, Passepartout bribes Fogg's previous servant to arrange his dismissal, so that Passepartout will be hired in his place. Actually winning admittance to the eccentrics requires a very strange deed, although walking around the Red Sea backward is not considered sufficiently bizarre—leading to the rejection of an American, Archibald Corsican (a character not present in the novel and added for the play).

At each stage of the play, fresh incidents are added from the novel. In Suez, the vengeful Archibald begins to pursue a literal vendetta against Fogg. (This explains the derivation of his surname, Corsican, since the island of Corsica had won fame for the social code that required a vendetta or the killing of anyone who had wronged the family honor, and Archibald blames Fogg for his rejection by the eccentrics.) Archibald, challenging Fogg to a series of duels with pistol and sabre, loses them all, making him an inept avenger.

In India, Aouda flees the Brahmins accompanied by her servant Nakahira; when captured, she agrees to suttee on the condition that Nakahira is allowed to return to her native Malayan Islands. Fix reveals his suspicions to Passepartout, and engages Fogg in a bidding war for the elephant. Aouda's rescue takes place as in the novel, with

---

7. Gérome, *L'Univers Illustré* (November 14, 1874), 723.

Adolphe d'Ennery, caricature by Verne's friend Nadar.

1874 advertisement.

the added assistance of Archibald, still following Fogg. In Bombay, they search for Aouda's only relation, Anardill; he had helped arrange for her marriage to the Rajah, when she was a sixteen-year-old full of ambition to rule. Instead she had found herself a widow who had never truly been a wife. Replacing her native dress, Aouda looks like a proper Englishwoman.

Passepartout finds that Anardill has died, but instead locates Nemea, Aouda's sister, also a new character in the play. Nemea indicates they need to leave India if Aouda is to be safe, and Fogg offers to take them to England. This also instantly establishes a rivalry between Passepartout and Archibald for Nemea's affection. Meanwhile, as in the book, detective Fix suspects Fogg of the bank robbery, but again departing from the book, it is Fix himself, in disguise, who takes the place of local antagonists in his ongoing attempts to delay Fogg until the arrival of an arrest warrant.

The novel's Chinese and Japanese episodes are completely replaced by Fogg's shipwreck in Borneo and visit to a cave of serpents. The creatures can only be controlled by their priestess, the very same Nakahira for whom Aouda was ready to sacrifice herself. When Fix steals Fogg's money bag, hoping to strand the travellers before more is spent and the 10% reward decreased, Archibald intervenes, having learned to esteem Fogg. Continuing to follow, Fix appears in blackface, speaking in dialect, on the train across the United States, and later on the *Henrietta* crossing the Atlantic. Unlike the novel, Indian motivations for attacking the train and hatred of white men are eloquently enunciated by their chief. Not only Passepartout, but also Aouda and Nemea, are taken their prisoner, and Fogg himself leads the rescue of all three.

On board the *Henrietta*, Fogg bribes the crew to compel Captain Cromarty (switching the name from the novel's Speedy to that of the officer in India) to sell him the vessel. Passepartout imagines that the gas-jet he had left on his room starts a fire that consumes London, a dream that parallels Axel's vision of evolution in Verne's novel *Voyage au centre de la Terre* (*Journey to the Center of the Earth*, 1864). Instead, Passepartout learns that the light was turned out by Margaret, his marriage-minded former fellow employee of the Eccentric Club who has joined them on the *Henrietta*. At last, she secures his grateful agreement to wed. Also on board is Fix, impersonating a cook, and Passepartout gets Fogg's money back from him.

Passepartout's nightmare of a burning London is echoed when the boiler of the *Henrietta* blows up, and the vessel sinks, with Fogg only rescued as Fix places handcuffs on him. The discovery of the extra day comes about, not because of sending for a minister to arrange the wedding with Aouda, but because of Fogg dispatching Passepartout to the bank to arrange for a draft to the other eccentrics. Fogg is allowed to proceed to London when Archibald pleads guilty to the robbery, and although others believe his confession, Nemea guesses the true nobility behind his action. Archibald, Passepartout, Aouda, and Nemea take the next train, following Fogg, and all are in suspense along with the club members. Fogg appears at the precise moment he is due, having taken the time to get a new frock and gloves. The play closes on the promise of a triple wedding: Fogg and Aouda, Passepartout and Margaret, and Archibald and Nemea.

In an interview with a journalist in 1893 in Amiens, Jules Verne himself had the opportunity to justify having the freedom to add characters which were not present in the novel. Asked about the character of Archibald Corsican, he explains that "He was necessary to 'feed' the plot. The audience needs what does not matter to the readers:

characters in conflict, in fight, in action."[8]

The play was performed more than 400 times at the Théâtre de la Porte St. Martin, something unheard of for a theatrical play; everyone in Paris wanted to see it. Alphonse Daudet, writer and critical reviewer, wrote in 1875 that he pitied the actors.

> By a mere chance I recently attended a performance of *Around the World* that I had not seen since the premiere, five months ago. I was struck to see that after so many representations the play was performed exactly as it was on the first night. The good actors, Dumaine, Vannoy, Alexandre, Lacressonière were still good and the bad ones have not changed either. For everybody, having gained more upright, more ease, their ridiculousness or qualities were more vividly outlined.
>
> The young Aouda and her sister still have the same false gestures, the same conventional cries. Mr. Lacressonière similarly still swings in an extra elegant way his small stick, lowering his shoulders and both elbows sticking to the body…
>
> What's most frightening to the poor Dumaine and his companions confined with him… is that after months and months, when they finally will get out of this play, they are threatened by catastrophe and a prison which may be more prolonged: *Children of Captain Grant* is the play the Porte Saint Martin plans to show after *Around the World*, which is also from a novel by M. Jules Verne, even more interesting than the adventures of brave Phileas Fogg. Certainly, we have nothing to say against such a success. It's the beginning of modern fairy plays using scientific tricks, indeed ingenious, and M. Jules Verne will soon have created a new genre in theater the same way he created one in literature.[9]

---

8. Pierre Dubois, "Avant Michel Strogoff," *Journal d'Amiens* (April 1, 1893), reprinted in Daniel Compère and Jean-Michel Margot, eds., *Entretiens avec Jules Verne* (Geneva : Slatkine, 1998), 78.

9. Alphonse Daudet, Pages inédites de critique dramatique (1874-1880), 1923. Bibliothèque nationale de France, Gallica <http://gallica.bnf.fr/ark:/12148/bpt6k57442726.r=.langEN>, retrieved March 31, 2011.

Around the World in 80 Days resumed later at the Théâtre du Châtelet and was on stage nearly 3,000 times between 1876 and 1940!

Around the World in 80 Days had no less success outside France. By 1875, the show had played in the Netherlands and across Europe. In Germany, *Around the World* was presented in Berlin and Frankfurt.[10] The Carltheater in Vienna had the play on stage without interruption for 108 performances; Viennese were enchanted by the almost magical change of sets and the scenic art. In Belgium, the play was presented at the theater of the Galeries Saint Hubert in February 1875 and ran more than 200 performances. Other theaters in Bruxelles also showed the play with the same success, and some other Belgian cities, like Ghent, in Flanders, had it on stage too.[11]

Following this triumph, Verne continued to work with d'Ennery. Between 1879 and 1882, they adapted two more Verne novels, the 1868 book *Les Enfants du capitaine Grant* (*The Children of Captain Grant*), and the more recent 1876 novel *Michel Strogoff* (*Michael Strogoff*). The fourth collaboration between Verne and d'Ennery included heroes from various Vernian novels, like Nemo, Ardan, Ox, and Lidenbrock, but was completely original.[12] This science fiction play, *Voyage à travers l'impossible* (*Journey Through the Impossible*), was performed in 1882. After having been lost for over a century, the North American Jules Verne Society published the first English translation in 2002, the first complete edition of the play in any country.[13]

Of these three shows, all appreciated by the public and the critics, *Michael Strogoff* came closest to the great success of *Around the World in 80 Days*, and sometimes superseded it; in the United States it became arguably more popular. In Paris, the expression, "It's Strogoff!," became a buzzword to describe the amazing and wonderful.

Around the World in 80 Days toured France, with all Frenchmen desirous of attending a show so praised by the newspapers. In the years

---

10. Roland Innerhofer, in K. Aman, H. Lengauer et K. Wagner, eds., *Deutsche Science Fiction 1870-1914* (Vienna: Böhlen, 1996), 53.

11. Philippe Burgaud, "Le Tour du Monde et les théâtres bruxellois," *Bulletin de la Société Jules Verne*, No. 70 (1984), 83.

12. Jean-Michel Margot, "Introduction," in Jules Verne, *Journey Through the Impossible* (Amherst, NY: Prometheus, 2003), 11-19.

13. Jean-Michel Margot, "Jules Verne, Playwright," *Science Fiction Studies*, 32 (March 2005), 150-162.

Program for the Théâtre du Châtelet presentation in 1905.

following World War I, a circular with the letterhead of MM. Gervais and Larroque, theatrical tour organizers, with exclusive privilege of the properties of the Théâtre du Châtelet, showed that *Around the World in 80 Days*, as well as *Michael Strogoff*, were shown in all major French cities.

It was these theatrical adaptations that Verne coauthored, not the original novels themselves, that made Jules Verne wealthy.[14] Verne could afford a steam and sail yacht in 1877, *Saint Michel III*, with a crew of ten. The *Saint-Michel III* replaced the *Saint-Michel II*, another boat he had just had built at the shipyards Abel Merchant, in Le Havre.[15]

After these achievements, Verne believed he had enough experience to write a play alone, and not share the authorship. In 1883, Verne adapted his novel of the same year, *Kéraban-le-têtu* (*Keraban the Inflexible*), and in 1887, turned over the adaptation of his 1885 novel, *Mathias Sandorf* to William Busnach and Georges Maurens. However, these two pieces were much less sucessful. Was the public too tired of these "pièces à grand spectacle"? Or were the chosen novels too difficult to adapt to the stage? Whatever the ultimate reason, certainly Verne's collaborations with d'Ennery always attracted audiences.

---

14. Jean-Michel Margot, "Introduction: Jules Verne—the Successful, Wealthy Playwright," in Jules Verne, *Mr. Chimp & Other Plays* (Albany, GA: BearManor Fiction, 2011), 5-29.
15. Philippe Valetoux, *En mer et contre tous* (Paris : Magellan & Cie, 2005).

Program for the Théâtre du Châtelet presentation in 1911.

The Kiralfy Brothers and Verne on the American Stage

When Bolossy Kiralfy (1847-1932) immigrated to the United States, he was only 24, but already had a career as an artist and dancer. Of Hungarian origin, he was born January 31, 1848 in Pest. He was on the stage by the age of four with his brother Imre (1845-1919), two years his senior, performing Hungarian dances. Encouraged by their parents, the two brothers studied with the most famous teachers. However, opportunities in Hungary were limited, and Kiralfy's father sought other places for his entire theatrical family. There were two other brothers, Roland (185 - ?) and Arnold (185?-1908), as well as three sisters, Haniola (1851-1889), Katie (185? -1924) and Emily (1855-1917); Hanolia became well-known as an accomplished ballerina.[16]

Departing for Germany, they taught dance classes and were on stage in Berlin and Munich in the early 1860s. Between 1865 and 1869, the family traveled between Brussels, London and Paris, alternating classes and performances. The Parisian stay of the Kiralfys in 1864 was important for several reasons. Until 1858 theaters could allow only a maximum of four characters playing together, in order not to compete with the Comédie française (French Comedy), the national theater of France and the world's longest established national theater.[17] However, in 1864, a decree of Napoleon III introduced the so-called "liberté des théâtres" (theatrical freedom) by removing all control, except the censorship of the plays.[18] The Kiralfys arrived as the Parisian theater managers were able to indulge their desire for great musical spectacles. Bolossy, Imre, and Haniola secured several contracts, mainly with the Théâtre des Variétés, but also with the Théâtre de la Porte Saint Martin, and the Châtelet. In the rest of France, they toured in musical spectacles. In early November, they were on stage in Caen, after successes in Le Havre.[19]

---

16. A website about the Kiralfy family is under construction: <www.kiralfy.net>.

17. After the death of the playwright Molière in 1673, his company of actors joined forces with another company and in 1680 was known as the Comédie française.

18. Thanks to this office and its archives, several Vernian plays that were considered lost were unearthed in the last few decades: *Keraban the Inflexible, Journey Through the Impossible,* and *Monsieur de Chimpanzé (Mister Chimpanzee)*; the latter was published in the Palik series in the volume, *Mr. Chimp & Other Plays.*

19. "Les danseurs hongrois," in *Le Passe-temps – Journal de l'entracte,* Caen, November 6, 1864, p. 2-3. A facsimile is available on Gallica at <http://gallica.bnf.fr/ark:/12148/bpt6k54501102/f2.image.langFR>, accessed March 31, 2011.

On stage at the Théâtre des Variétés, the Kiralfys witnessed the triumph of *La Belle Hélène* (*The Beautiful Helen*).[20] An operetta in three acts with music by Jacques Offenbach (1819-1880), the libretto was by Henri Meilhac and Ludovic Halévy. Offenbach became a good friend of the Kiralfys, and with his support, Bolossy and Imre attended classes at the Paris Opera under the direction of Mr. Barrez, director of ballet. Bolossy met the dancer and choreographer Arthur Saint-Leon (1821-1870) and the composer Léo Delibes (1836-1891). With Delibes, Bolossy learned to combine music and dance in a show, an essential combination for the rest of his career. About this time, Bolossy wrote, "There is no question that in Paris I acquired my training, not only in the finest ballet technique from Monsieur Barrez, but in the areas of production and management… My experience at the Théâtre de la Porte Saint Martin and at the Châtelet gave me the ability to produce big spectacular numbers."[21]

The Kiralfys became so famous that Leopold II, King of Belgium, asked Bolossy and Imre to organize the 1868 Brussels celebrations honoring the memory of Emperor Maximilian, who had died in Mexico in 1867; his widow was Leopold's sister. The reputation of the Kiralfy family spread beyond the boundaries of Europe, and they were asked many times by American theater directors to come to the United States. While the family was in London, Bolossy remained in Brussels and was visited by Samuel Colville (1825-1886), the famous American theater director. The financial incentives he offered to Bolossy, Imre, and Haniola impelled them, without consulting with their parents, to sign a contract. In May 1869, the family embarked at Liverpool for an Atlantic crossing aboard the *City of Antwerp* to New York.

Upon arrival, they discovered that Colville had sold the Kiralfy contract to another theater director, John Duff, a common practice in the United States and one which had no negative consequences for the Kiralfy family. They were expected to be part of a new show, *Hickory Dickory Dock*, full of sketches and pantomimes, with George L. Fox as

---

20. It was first performed on December 17, 1864, and was an instant success, enjoying an initial run of 700 performances. Robert Pourvoyeur, *Offenbach* (Paris: Seuil, 1994), 84ff.

21. Barbara Barker, *Bolossy Kiralfy, Creator of Great Musical Spectacles, an Autobiography* (Ann Arbor, MI: UMI Research Press, 1988), 73.

star.[22] Bolossy, Imre and Haniola had a solo dance, with her two little sisters in a secondary role, joined by eight other dancers. In this way, Americans discovered the famous Hungarians.

Bolossy and Imre Kiralfy realized that there was an opportunity to present major popular stage entertainment combining music, songs, dances and drama around a common theme with a hero or heroine, to make it interesting for the spectator. They also began to be known for the quality of their lighting, sets and stage equipment, which were manufactured and painted in Paris, London and Milan. The two brothers made regular visits to Europe for ideas.

Beginning in 1872, Imre and Bolossy Kiralfy produced musicals on their own. They first revived a great American success, *The Black Crook*, today considered the first piece of musical theater conforming to the modern notion of a "book musical."[23] The show began in August 1873 at Niblo's Garden, freshly rebuilt, a Broadway theater near Prince Street that had first opened in 1823. *The Black Crook*, with new ballets, and a huge crew of actors, then traveled from Broadway throughout the United States.[24]

In 1874, again at Niblo's, Imre and Bolossy staged *The Deluge*, inspired by the Bible.[25] Searching for another good musical, they believed a real plot was necessary to support the action, but found that American authors did not compose in that style. *Around the World in 80 Days* seemed to offer just what the Kiralfys needed; on November 29, 1874, a *New York Times* article echoed the London

---

22. Using the title of the well-known nursery rhyme, *Hickory Dickory Dock*, was a Broadway show at the Olympic Theater, with 110 presentations between May 18 and September 4, 1869. The play was written by George L. Fox (1825-1877), considered America's first great white-faced clown.

23. The book was by Charles M. Barras (1826-1873) and the music by Thomas Baker (1827-1903).

24. Niblo's Garden was established in 1823 as Columbia Garden, which in 1828 gained the name of the Sans Souci and was later the property of the coffeehouse proprietor and caterer William Niblo (? –1878). The large theater was twice burned and rebuilt.

25. Advertised as a "grand spectacular drama" but with "500 ballets and auxiliaries on stage," *The Deluge* was actually a musical pageant. The source was a French drama performed in Paris some ten years earlier that related stories from the Old Testament, including Adam and Eve, Cain and Abel, and the great flood. Gerald Martin Bordman, *American Musical Theatre* (New York: Oxford University Press, 1978), 39.

ROYAL PRINCESS'S THEATRE.

Sole Manager ... ... Mr. M. L. MAYER.

No. 73, Oxford Street.

ROUND THE WORLD IN 80 DAYS,

A NEW GRAND SPECTACULAR DRAMA

IN 18 TABLEAUX.

ADAPTED FROM

Messrs. A. D'ENNERY & J. VERNE'S

GREAT PARISIAN SUCCESS

"Le Tour du monde en 80 jours"

Produced under the Personal Direction

OF

Messrs. C. WEINSCHENK & M. L. MAYER.

An 1875 British program.

Times in praising the production in Paris. "It is not that the *Tour du Monde* shines by its dramatic conception or by its style, but the piece is at once so wholesome, original, and lively that there is not a family existing which need conceal the fact that it has seen it or wishes to see it, and at the same time not one which will not, from its eldest to its youngest member, enjoy its evening round the world."[26]

The first English adaptation of *Around the World in 80 Days* by Verne and d'Ennery was presented at London's Royal Princess Theatre in 1875. That same year, making use of the many contacts they had in Paris, Imre and Bolossy decided to acquire the exclusive rights to the Verne-d'Ennery show in America. To that effect, they sent their secretary Edmond Gerson with instructions to make a deal with the copyright owners, including the original music by Debillemont. The Kiralfys decided to copy all the sets and costumes of the show in Paris and hire the majority of the troupe playing at the Théâtre de la Porte Saint Martin, including part of the management. Because the production's size required huge facilities, the two brothers rented the New York Academy of Music, by then the largest theater in the city.

During the rehearsal period, Bolossy saw a newspaper advertisement for the Bowery Theater, announcing "Around the World in Eighty Days, the great spectacular and realistic drama, in six acts and ten tableaux, from the novel of Jules Verne." Having acquired the exclusive rights, the Kiralfys prepared to go to court, but found that legally they could not request an injunction before the play opened. That first evening, April 5, Imre and Bolossy were among the spectators at the Bowery Theater, and the brothers took notes. Although the Bowery show lacked the opulence the Kiralfys planned, the playscript was the same. The next day, an initial court decision suspended the Bowery show, and at the trial that followed, the director of the Bowery Theater was obliged to cancel it. Their competitor, seduced by the spectacle during a trip to Paris, had pirated the script by means of renting a box for enough performances to take down the text in its entirety.

---

26. "Foreign Gossip: The Paris correspondent of the London *Times* writes: 'Of all the Boulevard theaters, the Porte St. Martin is the one which has secured the greatest success with "Round the World," drawn from one of the last works of M. Jules Verne.'" *New York Times*, November 29, 1874.

The 1875 British program contained pages, accordion style, advertising Aouda's costumes.

In planning their production, the Kiralfys made several changes. For example, Archibald Corsican, the member excluded by the Eccentric Club, became O'Pake Miles, a former senator from New York. In his autobiography, Bolossy Kiralfy claimed that he asked Jules Verne to add a scene with a balloon. However, no mention of such a scene is found in reviews, nor is it in any script, and the recollection may be apocryphal. However, in Paris, one of the main attractions had been the elephant, and so Bolossy leased one of the famous Barnum elephants at $150 dollars per week, plus the salary of the keeper.

The first performance of *Around the World in 80 Days* took place August 26, 1875. (That very same day, yet another unauthorized competitor, directed by Augustin Daly at the Grand Opera House, closed its ten-day run; reviews had been tepid.[27]) At the premiere, the Kiralfy's show had five acts and eighteen tableaux, with numerous dancing interludes performed by the whole Kiralfy family, advertised as the "Famous Kiralfy Sisters." The production was a huge success.[28]

After the New York City run, the Kiralfys took their show across the United States. A whole train was rented with the elephant in the

---

27. *New York Times*, August 17, 1875.

28. *New York Times*, August 29, 1875.

last luggage car. From late October 1875 until June 1876, *Around the World in 80 Days* was performed in most of the major American cities.

Now the Kiralfys were wealthy, and the two brothers bought a beautiful house on Washington Square in New York City. They built a huge theater, the Alhambra Palace, in Philadelphia, but did not find the anticipated audience and were forced to sell at a major loss.[29] Returning to New York City, they resumed various shows, with such new ones as *Voyage dans la Lune* (*Trip to the Moon*), which premiered at Booth's Theatre on March 14, 1877. The show received a lukewarm critical reaction, the *New York Times* commenting that "the lack of one or two voices of the requisite charm and strength to interpret it was unpleasantly apparent last night. The ballet, however, left nothing to be desired, and, had the acting as well as the singing been equally good, M. Verne's play would be likely to have a prolonged run."[30] *Trip to the Moon* was actually an operetta by Offenbach, only capitalizing on the popularity of Verne's novels *De la Terre à la lune* (*From the Earth to the Moon*, 1865) and *Autour de la lune* (*Around the Moon*, 1869), but reviewers often mentioned the author rather than the composer in their reviews.

The Kiralfys again brought *Around the World in 80 Days* to Niblo's Garden in 1878 and 1880, with no less popularity and praise than before. During the latter run, the Kiralfys learned that Verne and d'Ennery's new play, *Michael Strogoff*, was a huge success in Paris and elsewhere in Europe.[31] As before, the Kiralfys corresponded with Verne and d'Ennery and obtained exclusive rights for the United States, and again rivals rushed to bring *Strogoff* to the stage. This time, Bolossy went to Paris to see the show, especially to note the differences between it and the book. In this way, in case he needed to go to court, he could delineate the distinctions between the stage and the novel, something those who only had access to the book could not do.

---

29. Kiralfy's Alhambra Palace was built in 1876, and later became Broad Street Theatre, and was demolished in 1937.
30. *New York Times*, March 15, 1875.
31. Three years before the Parisian show of *Michael Strogoff*, a dramatic spectacle, *Courier des Czaren*, based on the novel but not the play by Verne, had already been created in Pest (Hungary) and also played in the Carltheater in Vienna. See Roland Innerhofer, *Deutsche Science Fiction*, 53.

In the fall of 1881, *Michael Strogoff* was offered on stage to New York audiences at Aberle's Theater and at Booth's Theater. However, the true competition came from Massachusetts and the Boston Theatre, which opened its fall season with a great dramatic spectacle, *Michael Strogoff*. The Kiralfys met again there Samuel Colville, now the director of the theater, the same man who had been instrumental in bringing the brothers to America. The role of Michael Strogoff was played by the famous Anglo-American actor William Redmund (1850-1915), and the play was on stage or eleven weeks.[32]

Bolossy decided to make *Strogoff* even more dramatic than *Around the World*, with a considerable number of extras and grand scenic effects. With sumptuous sets, staging and inventive ballets, including over 100 remarkable dancers led by Bolossy, this staging was the only one to really appeal to the public, with the press comparing it favorably to the Boston version.

In 1883, the Kiralfys used electricity for the first time, in a show called *Excelsior*. The electric lamp had been patented in 1879, and the assistance of Thomas Edison (1847-1931) himself was secured. More than five hundred lamps were installed, with some placed in the costumes of the dancers.[33]

During the summer of 1885, the Kiralfys faced a serious problem. William Frederick "Buffalo Bill" Cody was touring with his show, *Buffalo Bill's Wild West*. Cody (1846-1917) was a soldier and bison hunter, an Iowa native who lived in Canada and Kansas before emerging as one of the most colorful figures of the West. Turning showman, he adapted his fame to tour Great Britain and Europe as well as the United States. Whenever *Around the World in 80 Days* and Buffalo Bill's shows were in the same town, he would come on stage and shoot blank bullets at the Indians that Fogg encountered in America. Buffalo Bill's own show was unstructured, and in exchange for his theatrical advice, Bolossy persuaded the hunter to stop disrupting his show.

Over the following years, Imre and Bolossy criss-crossed the United States with various musical productions, but *Around the World*

---

32. Eugene Tompkins & Quincy Kilby, *The History of the Boston Theatre, 1854-1901* (Boston: Houghton Mifflin, 1908). *Michael Strogoff* is described from page 283 to page 292.

33. Don B. Wilmeth, *The Cambridge Guide to American Theatre* (New York: Cambridge University Press, 2007), 372.

A stereogram, which when placed in a device, allows viewing a type of 3-D image.

in 80 Days was always a part of the trip. In September 1885, the staging in Boston for a limited time was so successful that it forced organizers to add matinées.[34]

In 1886, the two brothers split acrimoniously, an estrangement that endured for many years. Bolossy was still active as artistic director and producer of new musicals, but now Imre was a competitor, not only in the United States, but also in Great Britain. Bolossy traveled to Europe to select shows whose rights he could acquire for the United States. Invited by the French dramatist Victorien Sardou (1831-1908), from whom he had just acquired the rights to his play, *La Patrie* (*The Fatherland*), Bolossy was surprised to be introduced to d'Ennery, Verne, and Jules Massenet.[35] Verne and Sardou were long-time friends, and the first English translation of one of their collaborations, the 1861 play *Onze jours de siege* (*Eleven Days of Siege*), is included in another volume of the Palik Series, *Mr. Chimp & Other Plays*. Of the meeting with Sardou, d'Ennery, and Massenet, Bolossy noted in his memoirs that Verne, "in spite of a recent bullet wound that rendered him a semi-cripple and denied him his favorite pastime of sailing, was in a

---

34. "Stage and Concert," *Boston Daily Globe*, September 27, 1885, p.10.

35. Sardou wrote several plays that were made into popular 19th-century operas such as *La Tosca* (1887) on which Puccini's opera *Tosca* (1900) is based. Jules Émile Frédéric Massenet (1842 –1912) was a French composer best known for his operas. His compositions were very popular in the late 19th and early 20th centuries.

From left, Bolossy, Haniola, and Imre Kiralfy as shown on 1873 poster.

Advertisement for Bolossy's final achievement.

jovial mood and enjoyed exchanging barbed repartee with Massenet."[36] (Verne had been shot in 1886 by his brother's son, Gaston, who spent the rest of his life in an asylum.)

Bolossy decided to produce *Mathias Sandorf* in 1888, and Verne, pleased, aided Bolossy in securing exclusive American rights. At the request of Bolossy, Verne and William Busnach, co-author of the stage version, rewrote some scenes to fit the expectations of the American public.[37] However, Bolossy went further to make it a true blockbuster, multiplying the interludes with gymnasts, clowns, and musicians, adding two huge ballets, one with 120 dancers and the other with 200.

The American premiere of *Mathias Sandorf* was on August 18, 1888. The reviews were laudatory, with some reservations about the length of some interludes, and the noise emanating from backstage. The opportunity to listen today to a ballet written for the show exists on a portion of a 2010 CD release, *Masters of the Clarinet*.[38] As usual after the performances in New York City, Bolossy Kiralfy took *Mathias Sandorf* to other cities.

In 1890, back in New York, Bolossy again produced *Around the World in 80 Days* at Niblo's Garden, a new presentation but with the same success. He toured the show again throughout the United States, in Atlanta in 1892, in San Francisco in 1895, and in Baltimore, Washington and Boston in 1902.

At the turn of the century, great outdoor musical productions were emerging and Bolossy was one of their architects. Impressive scenes were built with pools where boats, gondolas, or wherries could be placed. In 1891, *King Solomon* had up to a thousand participants on stage, but soon this would be exceeded.[39] Invited to Europe in 1893, Bolossy created the spectacle *Orient* at the Olympia Theatre in London,

---

36. Barker, 130-131.

37. William Bertrand Busnach (1832 - 1907) was a French dramatist and novelist. He adapted several works of Zola to the stage and worked with Jacques Offenbach.

38. The Archeophone Records CD, *Masters of the Clarinet*, covered the period 1892-1920. On it were two songs written for the ballets of Bolossy Kiralfy's *Mathias Sandorf*, one played in 1888, and the other later. It is available at Archeophone Records, 4106 Rayburn Ct, Champaign, IL: http://www.archeophone.com/product_info.php?products_id=99, retrieved March 31, 2011.

39. *New York World*, June 29, 1891.

the largest ever worldwide, with 2500 people on stage, illustrative of the chivalry, pomp, and panoply of the 15th century.[40] After taking the production to Berlin, Bolossy presented the same show for the Paris International Exhibition of 1900. A portion was on water at the edge of the Bois de Boulogne, and to house this enormous undertaking, "The Giant Columbia Theatre" company was created, hosting 6,000 spectators. The splendors of ancient Byzantium, the mysterious kingdom of Fermirzah and London in the Fifteenth Century, were all offered in a spectacle that won Kiralfy approbation as the "Napoleon" of the stage.[41]

Orient was destined to be his crowning achievement. By this time cinema was emerging, and the shows Bolossy was planning were more and more expensive to create. There were no more international exhibitions to defray the costs. Without the wish to start a new career in filmmaking, he dedicated himself to his family and reading. Bolossy Kiralfy died in London, March 6, 1932, age 85.

---

40. Wilmeth, 372.
41. "Napoléon et Kiralfy," *Le Petit Parisien*, No. 8809 (July 27, 1899), 3.

The following pages reproduce a rare archival copy of an exact translation of the original Verne-d'Ennery play, prepared for the Kiralfy brothers, and copyrighted by them. As a publication, it received very limited distribution. Some modifications to the text were made by the Kiralfys before it was finally presented on the American stage, as noted in the Introduction.

PROLOGUE.

Tableau I.—A Wager of a Million.

ACT I.

Tableau II.—The Suez Canal. *Tableau III.*—An Indian Bungalow. *Tableau IV.*—

ACT II.

Tableau V.—A Room in an Hotel at Calcutta. *Tableau VI.* The Serpents' Grotto, Malay. *Tableau VII.*—The Fête of the Snake Charmers, Malay.

ACT III.

Tableau VIII.—Tavern at San Francisco. *Tableau IX.* The Train attacked upon the Pacific Railway. *Tableau X.* The Giants' Staircase.

ACT IV.

Tableau XI.—The Saloon of the Steamer Henrietta.
Tableau XII.—The Steamer 'Henrietta' at Sea.
Tableau XIII.—The Waif.

ACT V.

Tableau XIV.—At Liverpool. *Tableau XV.*—The Excentric Club House.

PROLOGUE.

A WAGER OF A MILLION.

Scene: A reading and card room in the Club of the Excentrics, in London. Other rooms open up from it. On each side sofas and arm-chairs. Whist tables at first entrance. In the centre, large oval table, strewn with newspapers. Chimney L. *with fire lighted. It is winter time. A clock above the door at the back. The large rooms are comfortably but not extravagantly furnished. A chandelier, hanging above the large table, and the candelabra on the chimney-piece, are lighted.*

SCENE I.

FLANAGAN, STUART, RALPH, *and other members of the club discovered. They are warming themselves by the fire, and they glance through pamphlets and newspapers whilst they are talking.*

RALPH. Well, and when is our new club-house to be finished?

FLAN. A house! my dear Ralph. You mean a palace.

RALPH. Well then, call it a palace, if you like. It is really too bad for gentlemen like those who have founded the Excentric Club to have to put up with a den like this.

STUART. Ralph is right! Why, we eat, we drink, we are housed in short, we live like everybody else! May old England forgive us, but there are wool-sellers and brewers in London, who are more excentric than we are. There is the butcher Nordisson, for instance, when he has sold his meat at his stall in the city, well, he jumps into his open carriage, drawn by four horses, and with his arms bare, and with his apron tied round his waist, he drives home to his house in Piccadilly. Now there is an excentric butcher for you!

FLAN. Everybody can't be a butcher!

RALPH. No, but one ought to distinguish one's self from other people.

FLAN. Never fear, my dear Ralph, in our new palace, you will have no cause for complaint—at least as far as the house is concerned.

STUART. And it will cost ten millions—that's tolerably excentric, to begin with.

RALPH. Pooh! there are fifty of us to pay for that fancy.

STUART. And it is to be finished?

FLAN. In three months—The upholsterers are already at work.

STUART (*frightened*). What do mean, the upholsterers? Are there to be carpets then?

FLAN. Yes, of course—since there are floors.

STUART. And curtains!

FLAN. Of course—since there are windows.

STUART. And ceilings, and doors, and staircases? I shouldn't be surprised if there are staircases.

FLAN. Undoubtedly.

STUART (*falling back dumfounded.*) With steps?

FLAN. With steps—why, of course. You may be as excentric as you like, but you must have windows to give you light, and doors to obtain access to the rooms, and staircases to go up stairs.

STUART. Yes, yes—it's true—and if it were not for this miserable staircase—and the steps—especially the steps—

RALPH. I say, gentlemen, of course we shall give a fête for the inauguration of this palace.

FLAN. Yes, an excentric ball, preceded by a dinner that will cost five hundred thousand francs.

STUART. Without the wine.

FLAN. Of course. Moreover, we shall appoint a committee to settle on the *menu*.

RALPH. By the bye gentlemen, have they settled on the election of this man from the United States, Archibald Corsican?

FLAN. His qualifications were not considered to be sufficiently high, and on the recommendation of the Secretary to the Committee, Phileas Fogg, he was blackballed. (*At this moment, the door at the back opens, and* PASSEPARTOUT *in a handsome livery appears.*)

PASSE. (*in a solemn voice*). Dinner is on the table.

STUART (*contemptuously.*) Oh! dinner, dinner!—to dine like everybody else!

Original English page 6

RALPH. At all events, they have sent for some Lake Erie ice.

PASSE. *(solemnly.)* Yes, your honour, and they have taken care to send it from the south-east extremity of the lake, where the quality is the best.

[*The members of the club exeunt at the back, and* PASSEPARTOUT *sinks down on a divan.*

SCENE II.

PASSEPARTOUT *afterwards* MARGARET.

PASSE. To wait on one excentric, that may be all very well, but fifty——no! I have had enough of it, and then, when I say excentric, I am not sure! For if these gentlemen were really excentric, they would wait upon their servants, they'd do our rooms and brush our clothes.

MAR. (*showing herself at the door* L.) Is there anybody here?

PASSE. (*who remains seated.*) Yes, there is somebody. There is I.

MAR. (*entering.*) Then I may come in.

PASSE. Miss Margaret, your place is in the laundry. What do you want here?

MAR. I have come to ask you Monsieur Passepartout for a decided answer. Do you want to marry me—yes or no?

PASSE. (*leaving his chair to take possession of an arm-chair.*) No!

MAR. But you promised me——

PASSE. (*in an evasive manner.*) My dear.

MAR. Am I not to your taste?

PASSE. Yes!

MAR. Shouldn't I make a good little wife?

PASSE. Excellent.

MAR. You are a good Frenchman—I am a good Englishwoman——

PASSE. If you were Chinese, I should still reply No, no—again and again No! Now listen to me. Until now I have led a tolerably excited life—now in the service of one person—now in the service of another. I have been in twenty places, without finding a single good one, and I have travelled in twenty countries without settling anywhere. Now I am tired, broken down, used up——and I have made up my mind to take rest.

Mar. Very well then—let's get married.
Passe. Don't I tell you that I want rest——
Mar. Well.
Passe. That I want to take root somewhere——in a good soil, exposed to the sun——
Mar. *(planting herself before* Passepartout.*)* That's exactly it—Here's the good soil, well exposed to——
Passe. Too much exposed——Margaret, I am not made of the stuff, or rather of the iron, out of which husbands are manufactured. Besides, I am going to leave the club.
Mar. Leave the club?
Passe. Yes, it is beyond my strength to have to answer all the bells here. There is too much work here. I want a special place.
Mar. And you have found it?
Passe. And I have found it.
Mar. With whom?
Passe. With Mr. Phileas Fogg.
Mar. The gentleman who comes here every day regularly, at the same hour, at the same minute—who comes in by this door—who takes three steps forward, gives his hat with his right hand, his cane with his left—who then hands his great coat, sits down, holds his two hands like this, and his two feet so——and remains motionless until someone brings him his newspaper?—A regular piece of mechanism.
Passe. I am not sorry to have to wait upon a piece of mechanism.
Mar. But he is a man who goes by a spring, and has to be wound up every day.
Passe. The winding up has nothing to do with me.
Mar. I thought he had a servant—John Foster, by name?
Passe. That's to say, John Foster had him for a master—but I have bought the master.
Mar. Bought the master?
Passe. Yes. I went to see John Foster—I said to him " what do you want for your master?" " A thousand francs," said he to me. " Will five hundred do?" " No," replied John, " he is worth more than that." " Eight Hundred?" " Well, for your sake, Passepartout." " Many thanks John." ——And I paid him eight hundred francs—all my savings are gone, but I have got the gentleman whom I wanted.
Mar. Well—and John Foster?

Original English page 8

PASSE. Well—John had no more to do than to get himself dismissed. That was not such an easy matter with Mr. Fogg —who is not easily moved. Foster first of all neglected to bring his clothes—Mr. Fogg said nothing. Then Foster broke two mirrors—the first voluntarily, and the second on purpose——Still Mr. Fogg said nothing. The case became desperate. Luckily, this morning—this very morning—Foster brought Mr. Fogg his shaving water. Mr. Fogg rang for Foster. "John," said he in his calmest tones, "John," it was settled between us that my shaving water should always be thirty-five degrees in winter—this water is only thirty-four degrees——From this morning, seventeen minutes past eleven, you are no longer in my service." And that's how the phlegmatic gentleman comes into my service.

MAR. But suppose you don't suit him, Passepartout?

PASSE. He suits me—and that is enough for me, Margaret.

MAR. Then you have quite settled?

PASSE. What?

MAR. You won't take me for your wife, my little Passepartout?

PASSE. No, Margaret, little Passepartout has no intention of passing under your caudine forks.

MAR. Passepartout! Passepartout! I shall do something desperate.

PASSE. Do what you like!

MAR. I am offered a situation in America—— I shall go to America.

PASSE. A pleasant journey!

MAR. Oh, here's someone coming.

PASSE. It's my master.

MAR. Your future master?

PASSE. Oh, no, no! I have paid for him——He is mine!

[MAR. *runs off* R. PASSE. *rises from his chair.*

SCENE III.

PASSEPARTOUT. FOGG.

FOGG *enters* L, *walks with a mechanical step, sits down close to the table, on which the newspapers are laid, his body erect, bearing his head high, his feet together, like those of a soldier who presents arms. He takes hold of a large newspaper, which he begins to read.*

PASSE. (*aside, watching him.*) What a marvel of precision!—How well he is oiled—how well he works.

MAR. Oh, it's splendid—it's splendid? [*Exit.*

PASSE. (*aside.*) Now let's arrange matters. (*Aloud*). Sir, I am the valet who has been mentioned to you.

[FOGG *lowers his newspaper and looks at* PASSEPARTOUT *without making any gesture.*

FOGG. You are French, and your name is John?

PASSE. Jean, if you please Sir, John Passepartout——a nickname which is justified by my natural aptitude for getting out of any scrape.

FOGG. Passepartout suits me——Besides, you have been several years in the club, and you have given satisfaction.

PASSE. Allow me to add that I know all your habits, Sir. ——Rise at eight o'clock—tea and toast at 8. 23—letters at 9. 35—barber at seven minutes to ten—cupboard B, drawer H for the trousers—cupboard S, drawer K for the waistcoats—shaving water 35 degrees in winter, and 17 degrees in summer. In short, I know all the arrangements of the house, lighted and warmed by gas, consisting of five rooms and three closets, in Saville Street—and you will not have to tell me anything—

FOGG (*interrupting him*). You know the terms.

PASSE. I know.

FOGG. Good, what time is it?

PASSE. (*pulling out an enormous frying-pan from his pouch*). Forty-seven minutes past six.

FOGG. You are slow.

PASSE. Pray forgive me—it's an escapement watch.

FOGG. You are four minutes slow—but no matter. It will suffice to bear in mind the discrepancy. From this moment—fifty-one minutes past six—in the evening of Thursday, the third of October, 1872, you are in my service. Go!

[*At this moment Fogg unfolds his newspaper, which, according to the English custom, is never cut, and* FOGG *disappears behind the immense sheet, which measures several yards square.*

PASSE. (*watching his master*). I wait here for your orders, Sir.—Here I am, tranquil at last, and sure of no end of rest.

SCENE IV.

Fogg, Flanagan, Stuart, Ralph, Sullivan, *and other members of the Club. They enter by door at back.*

Stuart (*to* Sullivan). By-the-bye, my dear Sullivan, how about that affair of the two millions, which was stolen a fortnight ago from the Bank of England. You are Under Governor, and you ought to be able to tell us all about it.

Ralph. Well, I am afraid that the Bank will lose its money.

Sul. I hope, for my part, that, sooner or later, we shall catch the thief. Inspectors of police—very clever fellows—have been sent to Liverpool, to Glasgow, to Havre, to Suez, to Brindisi, to New York, and a week ago the Metropolitan Police despatched to them the description of two individuals, well dressed, of good manners, who were seen wandering about round the paying counter the very day that the theft was committed.

Ralph. Oh, as to descriptions—all descriptions of persons are alike.

Sul. In any case, the detective's zeal is certain to be considerably spurred, for the Bank of England has promised them ten per cent. of whatever sum may be recovered.

Stuart. Two hundred thousand francs if they recover the two millions! By Jove, it would be an excentric idea to run after the thief—if it were worth while.

Flan. In the first place, it is not a thief.

Sul. How do you mean—not a thief? This individual, who has carried off two millions of bank notes—

Flan. No, it's a sharper.

Fogg (*from behind a newspaper*). The *Times* declares that it is a gentleman.

Stuart. Who said that?—Why, Mr. Fogg.

All. Ah, Mr. Fogg!

> [*The newspaper is lowered.* Fogg *appears. He rises and coldly bows to his fellow members, who bow to him in return.*

Original English page 11

STUART. Well, for my part, I believe that the thief will get clear away.

FLAN. Nonsense! There isn't a single country in which the man could take refuge.

STUART. Indeed!

FLAN. Why—where can he go to?

STUART. I don't know—but, after all, the world is big enough.

FOGG. It was formerly.

STUART. What do you mean by formerly? Has the earth grown smaller?

FOGG. Much smaller; since it is traversed now ten times faster than it was twenty years ago. And this will much facilitate the flight of the gentleman in question.

STUART. I must confess, Mr. Fogg, that's a very droll way of yours of saying that the earth has grown less—so that now you can go round the world in three months.

FOGG. In eighty days you mean.

SUL. That's true, gentlemen—in eighty days—since the section between Rothal and Allahabad has been opened up on the Central Indian Railway.

STUART. Eighty days? Yes, that's all very well, but that doesn't make any allowance for bad weather, shipwreck, trains running off the lines, explosions—

FOGG. Making allowance for all.

STUART. In theory you are right, Mr. Fogg, but in practice—

FOGG. I am right in practice, too, Mr. Stuart.

STUART. I should like to see you do it.

FOGG. You can if you like—let's start together.

STUART. Heaven forbid! But I'd willingly wager two hundred thousand francs that the journey would be impossible on those conditions.

FOGG (*to* STUART). It is quite possible.

STUART. Why don't you do it, then, Mr. Fogg? Why don't you make this journey in eighty days?

FOGG. I will if you like.

SUL. But when?

FOGG. At once.

ALL. At once?

FOGG. I have a small fortune of two millions, gentlemen. Will you four bet me one half of that?

SUL. One million—which you may lose by five minutes' delay?

FOGG. I don't believe in delay.

RALPH. But accident?

FOGG. There is no such thing as accident.

FLAN. But observe, Mr. Fogg, that these eighty days to go round the world represent the minimum.

FOGG A minimum well employed is all sufficient.

RALPH. But in order not to go beyond it, you will have to jump with mathematical precision out of the railways into the steamers, and off the steamers into the railway carriages again.

FOGG. Well, then, I shall jump with mathematical precision.

SUL. Is this a joke?

FOGG (*rising*). I never joke, when the subject is so serious as a wager. I will bet you, gentlemen, one million, that I will go round the world in eighty days, that is to say, in 1920 hours, or 115,200 minutes.

All. Done.

FOGG. Done. The Dover train starts at 8.45. I shall take it.

STUART. This very evening?

FOGG. This very evening. I have a million on deposit at Baring Brothers—that will be my stake. The other million I shall take with me.

STUART. Take it with you on your journey?

FOGG. Yes, and spend it too, if necessary, gentlemen—in other words, there shall be no obstacles on my path. (*Taking a pocket book out of his pocket, and consulting an almanack*) Well, gentlemen, as to-day is Thursday, the 3rd of October, I must be back in the Club on Sunday, the 22nd of December, before the last stroke of nine has sounded on that clock.

FLAN. No, no, no—not here, but in the new palace which we shall inaugurate on that very night.

STUART. And we'll pay for the fête out of the million which—

FOGG. Which, gentlemen, you will lose.

[FOGG *rings the bell. Enter a club waiter.*

FOGG. Send my new servant.

SCENE V.

The same. PASSEPARTOUT..

FOGG. Passepartout—you have got seventeen minutes to get to my house. There are my keys—in my room there is a cupboard—

PASSE. Cupboard F.

FOGG. You will open it. On the tray—

PASSE. Tray letter K.

FOGG. You will find a travelling bag, already packed. You will take it, and you will bring it here.

PASSE. (*astonished*). A travelling bag?

FOGG. A travelling bag, always packed, in case I go away.

PASSE. (*with terror*). Then do you ever go away, sir?

FOGG. Yes—we are going round the world.

PASSE. (*crying out*). Round the—round the—round the world? (*He sinks into an arm-chair.*).

FOGG. No boxes—no parcels—we will buy all that we want on our way.

PASSE. (*in a hesitating and stupid manner*). Round the world?—And I have bought him in order to get rest.

FOGG. Go!—You have already wasted a minute.

PASSE. (*at the door*). Ah! If I hadn't paid my eight hundred francs for you, I'd soon send you in my little bill.

[*Exit in despair.*

SCENE VI.

Same, with the exception of PASSEPARTOUT.

STUART. Well, Mr. Fogg, we'll give you time to make your preparations.

FOGG. I am always ready, gentlemen. I have fifty-five minutes left, and twenty-two will be enough for me to get to the station. Gentlemen, it is the time for our usual game Pray sit down.

All. Let's sit down.

Curtain.

UN QUAI DU CANAL A SUEZ

The Port of the Suez Canal

ACT I.

TABLEAU II.

A Quay on the Suez Canal at Suez.

A Square at Suez—To the L. *a Café, with tables and curtains in the Turkish style. To the* R. *the Offices of* MUSTAPHA PASHA, *Governor of the town. At the back is the quay of the Suez Canal, used as a landing place. At the back the Canal curves obliquely. Ships at anchor, barks, dredging machines, &c. At the extreme back, the plains of Arabia, closed up by mountains,. Europeans and Fellahs walk up and down on the quay, and in the square.*

SCENE I.

MUSTAPHA PASHA. FIX.

MUSTAPHA *comes out of his bureau. He is elegantly dressed like a European.* FIX. *entering* L. *walks up to him.*

MUS. Go, Sir.
A SECRETARY. Yes, Monsieur le Gouverneur.
FIX (*bowing*). Ah! Monsieur le Gouverneur.
MUS. It is you, Mr. Fix.
FIX. Yes, your Excellency. I have been recommended to you by the English Government, but your Excellency has no information to give me.
MUS. None, Sir. No suspicious looking stranger has been seen in our province, nor has any disembarked at Suez.
FIX. That's too true, your excellency. I have been here for a fortnight, and I never leave this quay. I scrutinize the passengers of all the steamers in my endeavour to recognize the thief of the Bank of England, and I discover nothing—nothing.

Mus. You must be a little patient, Sir; thieves are not always in a hurry to get taken. By-the-bye, you know that the packet, the Mongolia, was signalled yesterday, off Port Saïd. It can't be long before she is in.

Fix. And the Mongolia comes direct from Brindisi?

Mus. From Brindisi, where she fetched the Indian mails at five o'clock on Saturday evening.

Fix. And she goes to Bombay?

Mus. Direct.

Fix. But she doesn't stop at Suez.

Mus. Only one hour—only just long enough to take in coals. But, in truth, with the very incomplete details which were sent you from London, I don't know how you could recognize the person in question, even if he happened to be on board the Mongolia.

Fix. Suspicion points especially to two individuals, who were observed to remain for a long time, near the paying counters at the Bank. I have got their description, but it isn't altogether on that, that I count, your Excellency. As for sharpers of this class—you scent them, rather than see them. What we detectives require most is a good nose.

Mus. Well, here's a splendid chance for making use of it—especially as the reward offered by the Bank is very attractive.

Fix. True, your Excellency, the Bank does these things well. Ten per cent. on the sum brought back, that means two hundred thousand francs if I secure the two millions stolen, and, do you know, I have something like a presentiment that my man is on board the Mongolia.

Mus. Really! And if he is there, what shall you do?

Fix. Your Excellency will, perhaps, not object to arrest him?

Mus. I arrest an English subject, who, perhaps, may not be the thief? Why, do you want to make the Khedive quarrel with Her Gracious Majesty?

Fix. Well, then, in that case, I shall immediately telegraph, begging them to send me a warrant of arrest, of which I can make use as soon as my thief shall set foot on an English colony.

Mus. But in that case you will follow him.

Fix. Until the end of the world, if need be. Two hundred thousand francs, and the honour!

Original English page 16

SCENE II.

The Same. ARCHIBALD.

ARCHIBALD CORSICAN *enters* R., *and walks up and down the quay. He has a telescope in his hand, and looks out in the direction of the Canal.*

MUS. *(perceiving him).* Ah! There's a gentleman who is awaiting the arrival of the Mongolia with as much impatience as you.

FIX. Is he a rival?

MUS. No, don't be afraid—but he is an original character. (*To* ARCHIBALD, *who walks towards him*). Good day, Mr. Archibald Corsican, citizen of the United States, &c.

ARCH. And the most impatient man in the world, your Excellency.

MUS. But why?

ARCH. Because this steamer doesn't come in, and it brings me, I hope, the news of my election to the Excentric Club in London.

MUS. Then you are very anxious to become a member of this singular club?

ARCH. Very.

MUS. What have you done to entitle you to membership?

ARCH. I have been round the red sea on foot.

MUS. Well, but——

ARCH. Yes, but I did it backwards.

MUS. Backwards—What was the use of that?

ARCH. Pray where would the excentricity be, if it were of any use?

MUS. That's true—and frankly, if you were not received after that, it would be a very hard case for the searchers after originality.

ARCH. That's my opinion.

MUS. I am quite sure that was not the way you went to London a fortnight ago.

ARCH. No, it certainly was not.

MUS. But you came back very quickly.

ARCH. Oh, I only just had time to go and get a large sum from the Bank.

FIX. *(aside listening.)* To get a large sum from the Bank!—What does he mean by that. *(Aloud.)* I beg your pardon, Sir,—then you were in London?——

ARCH. On the 17th of September last.
FIX. (*looking at* MUSTAPHA.) The 17th.——
MUS. Dear me! but that is exactly the day when two millions where stolen from the Bank.
ARCH. Exactly. And the thief and I both left it with an enormous sum——only the thief didn't do as I did— leave a receipt.
MUS. Oh!—mere forgetfulness.
ARCH. Yes—mere forgetfulness.
MUS. But if you were so impatient to get an answer from the Club, why did you come back here, and why didn't you wait for it in London?
FIX. True—Why not?
ARCH. Oh, that's an idea of mine. I don't want to live in London until I can put on my card, " Member of the Excentric Club."
FIX (*aside*). So, so. (*Aloud, looking* ARCHIBALD *in the face*). True, that gives a certain notoriety, and then inquisitive people cease to ask who you are.
ARCH. (*turning his back to him*) Precisely, Sir.
FIX (*aside*). Let's see, now. (*Pulling some papers out of his pocket, he consults them while watching* ARCHIBALD.) But he is like the first description—we shall meet again!
            [*Whistling of the boat heard.*
MUS. The packet.
ARCH. My letter, without doubt.
    [*Both run to the landing-place. At this moment the steamer is seen gliding between the two banks of the Canal, It stops at the landing-place. At the back of the stage, passengers disembark, and are hustled by fellahs, who seize their trunks.* ARCH. *jumps on board across the parapet of the quay.* FIX. *close to the gangway, scrutinizes all the passengers who disembark. Whistle from the engine. Cries of the fellahs.*

SCENE III.

MUSTAPHA. FIX. PASSEPARTOUT.

MUSTAPHA *avoiding the crowd is seated* L., *and is reading the* " *Figaro.*"

PASSE. So, here I am in Egypt—the country of Potiphar's wife. So I am going to see Egyptians, Dancing girls, Pachas,

Turks, real Turks, with turbans, plaited trousers, and wearing a full sun in their backs. But first of all, let me see about the commissions my master has given me—to buy some shirts and some handkerchiefs, and to have the passport viséed.

Fix (*coming back, after he has seen all the passengers disembark.*) Nobody on board at all like my man. In that case I must stick to my American.

Passe. (*perceiving him*). Oh, here's a gentleman who will show me the way. (*To* Fix.) Sir.

Fix. What?

Passe. Will you be kind enough to tell me, Sir, where I can get this passport viséd? (*Showing the passport*).

Fix. A passport? Allow me—I am very fond of reading passports.

Passe. Oh, pray do as you please.

Fix (*looking through the paper, aside*). Dear me! Dear me! But this is just like my second description.

Passe. Well, Sir?

Fix. This passport is not yours?

Passe. No, it is my master's.

Fix. Mr. Phileas Fogg?

Passe. Yes, yes! A master that I bought, and who made me start in great haste, I can tell you that.

Fix (*aside*). He is a chatterbox, good! (*Aloud*) Well, go on.

Passe. Now, what I wanted, was a sedentary and comfortable life, and he makes me run about from town to town, from country to country, stopping nowhere, throwing money about broadcast, to get on the quicker.

Fix (*aside.*) But this is just like a man who is running away.

Passe. And we have to go on in this way without luggage.

Fix. Without luggage?

Passe. Yes, but we buy all we want on our way.

Fix. To be able to travel in that way he must be very rich.

Passe. I should think he is, indeed—for he carries about with him an enormous sum in fine bank notes, all bran new.

Fix (*aside*). It is not the American—this must be the real individual.

Original English page 19

PASSE. Why, just fancy, he has promised a prize of twenty thousand francs to the men in the engine-room of the Mongolia, if we arrive at Bombay twenty-four hours before our time.

FIX (*aside*). Twenty thousand francs!—That's two thousand francs off my share—the blackguard!

PASSE. (*about to go away.*) But here I am, chattering.

FIX. (*detaining him.*) Is it long since you have known your master?

PASSE. Long?——I only went into his service forty-five minutes before we left.

FIX. And do you know why he left?

PASSE. On account of a great wager which he made.

FIX. Dear me!—a wager. Well, I will introduce you to the Governor, His Excellency Mustapha Pacha.

PASSE. A Pacha! Ah, ah! Then I shall see a real Pacha. [MUS. *comes forward at this moment.*

FIX. Here he is.

PASSE. What do you mean?—-That gentleman? But where's his turban and his sun? Does he only put them on when he goes to a masked ball?

FIX. (*aside.*) (*To* PACHA.) Your Excellency—I have found my man.

MUS. What do you mean?—This fellow?

FIX. No, his master, whose passeport I have here.
[*looks at his description.*

MUS. (*taking the passport.*) Mr. Phileas Fogg wishes to have his passport vis.

PASSE. If you have no objection, Pacha.

MUS. But he must attend in person, in order that his identity may be established.

PASSE. What, is that necessary?

MUS. Indispensable.

PASSE. Pacha—I will go and look for my master.
[FIX *keeps in the back-ground, and pulls the description out of his pocket.*

SCENE IV.

The same. FOGG. ARCHIBALD.

FOGG *and* ARCHIBALD *appear together on the gangway, by means of which the passengers disembark from the Mongolia.*

The gangway is narrow. They run against each other in passing. ARCHIBALD *rushes forward roughly.* FOGG *approaches with measured foot-steps.*

ARCH. (*to* MUS.) Oh, your Excellency, the wretches!—miserable John Bulls!—they have blackballed me.

[*showing a letter*

ARCH (*in a rage.*) They have considered me unworthy to figure in their idiotic society.——One of them—a Mr. Fogg—Fig—Fag—Fog, Phileas Fogg, has turned them all against me—I am dishonoured. (*Sits down at a Café, and knocks over a table and two chairs.*)

PASSE. (*pointing to* MUSTAPHA.) Here's the governor, Sir,—he requires your presence.

FOGG (to PASSEPARTOUT.) And the purchases I told you to make?

PASSE. I have not had time yet.

FOGG. But make haste, my friend——the steamer is going to start.

PASSE. (*exit* R.) Perhaps I shall come across a real Turk after all.

FIX. (*aside.*) He looks like a scoundrel.

MUS. (*aside.*) He looks like a very honest fellow.

FOGG (to MUSTAPHA.) His Excellency, Mustapha Pacha.

MUS. It is you, Sir, who wishes to have this passport visé'd?

FOGG. It is I.

MUS. You know that this formality as regards passports is no longer necessary?

FOGG. I know, but nevertheless, I should like to have mine visé'd, and I am ready to pay the fee.

MUS. Very good, Sir—Your name is Phileas Fogg?

[FOGG *bows slightly.*

ARCH. (*getting up in a rage.*) Phileas Fogg. (FOGG *bows.* A member of the Excentric Club? (FOGG *bows.*) Well, Sir I am Archibald Corsican, of New York, State of New York (FOGG *bows*). And I have been put up at the Excentric Club, and I have been blackballed, (FOGG *bows*) and blackballed,—thanks to the ill-will of a certain Phileas Fogg, who didn't consider me worthy to take a seat by his side——me, a man who had just performed the journey round the Red Sea backwards.

Fogg (*ironically.*) Backwards!—That wasn't sufficient, Sir. Ah! if you had made the journey hopping—on one leg—then, perhaps——

Arch. (*in a rage*). Sir—

Fogg (*coldly.*) Sir.

Mus. Gentlemen.

Arch. I beg your pardon, Sir.

Fogg. I beg your pardon, sir—I have made a wager to go round the world in eighty days—in other words, in one hundred and fifteen thousand, two hundred minutes—you have made me lose two, that's enough.

Arch. (*restraining himself*). One moment, Sir, pray hear me, Mr. Phileas Fogg. I intend to put up again, and this time, I hope, with a better chance. What do you imagine your fellow members would think of a man, who, considering that you had grossly insulted him, should kill you, should have you dried, turned into a mummy, and put in a box of sandal-wood, taking care to have you well wrapped up, like a cotemporary of the ancient Pharaohs?

Fogg. My friends would certainly think you sufficiently excentric, but they would scarcely be able to admit you to the club.

Arch. And pray, why?

Fogg. Because they would seem by this means to pay the individual who, by killing me, helped them to gain their wager against me.

Arch. And if, after having killed you, I nevertheless enabled you to gain your wager.

Fogg. It seems to me that would be rather difficult.

Arch. And, nevertheless, it is perfectly simple. Killed, and quite mummified, I should carry you about as luggage, and completing myself, your journey round the world, I should bring you back to London within the appointed time—dead, but victorious. Do you understand now?

Fogg. Perfectly. Yes, you would certainly have a very good chance of being accepted by my friends.

Arch. Ah!

Fogg. But you would have as great a chance of being killed by me!

Arch. That we shall see.

Fogg. Whenever you please.

Original English page 22

Arch. In the court-yard of my hotel we shall be perfectly alone.

Fogg. I am at your orders.

Arch. I go before you.

Fogg And I follow you.

[*The two exeunt* L.

SCENE VI.

Mustapha. Passepartout. Fix.

Mus. If the detective is not mistaken, this Fogg is a strange kind of thief.

Fix (*entering hastily*). I have sent off my despatch—Well, your Excellency, where is my man?

Mus. Your man is just engaged in a duel.

Fix. In a duel?

Mus. Yes, with an American—who has picked a quarrel with him.

Fix. Good—good. I don't want him to be killed, but a little scratch which would keep him in bed for a week——

Passe. (*entering.*) Well, I have got all we want; here we are, provided with shirts and handkerchiefs, in the latest fashion——(*he holds up impossible shirts with paintings of animals, of ibises, crocodiles, and inscriptions.*) That's all I could find—but it seems that it is what's worn here. I shall keep this one for myself. (*Looking round about him.*) But where's my master?

Fix. Your master, my lad—at this moment he is fighting a duel.

Passe. Fighting a duel! Oh, good Heaven! and my eight hundred francs. Suppose they kill him.

Fix. Let's hope that he will only be wounded, and that he will get off with a week's confinement to his room.

Passe. A week?——But that's more than is necessary to ruin him.

Fix. (*aside.*) That's just the time that I want to get my warrant.

Passe. Where is he—Where is he fighting? Mr. Fogg, Mr. Fogg! Ah!——Thank Heaven—here he is.

SCENE VII.

The same. Fogg *and* Archibald.

Arch. (*with his left arm bandaged.*) Wounded!—I am wounded—But we will have it over again in a week.

Fogg. In eight minutes I shall have left.

Arch. Then I shall go with you.

Fix. (*aside.*) And so shall I.

Fogg. As you please, Sir.

Arch. Until I have killed you, Sir

Fogg. Or until you have been killed by me, Sir——Sum total of the hours spent till now, 158.

Fix. Total of the sums spent by my thief, about 23,000 francs.

Fogg. So I have 1,762 hours left.

Fix. He has still 1,977,000 francs, of which 197,000 for my share.

[*Bell heard on board the boat, with a whistle of the engine and the puffing of the steam. The crowd rushes on the quay.*

Fogg (*to* Passe.) You have not forgotten anything, Passepartout?

Passe. I assure you, Sir, that I have forgotten nothing, neither here nor in London—where I locked up everything before leaving. I looked up everything before leaving. I locked up everything, and I put out all the lights. (*Uttering a tremendous cry*). Oh, great Heavens!

Fogg (*coming back*). What is the matter, Passepartout?

Passe. The matter, Sir!—I have just recollected that I forgot—

Fogg. What?

Passe. I forgot to put out the gas-light in your bed-room.

Fogg Then, my lad, it is still burning—at your expense.

Passe. At my expense—and we are going round the world!

All embark. Steamer leaves. Curtain.

TABLEAU III.

A Bungalow in an Indian Forest.

The Stage represents a Bungalow, a sort of ruined caravanserai. The country is seen across the walls, which are crumbled half away, and covered with plants. The Bungalow is deserted when the curtain rises. The sun is sinking.

SCENE I.

Aouda. Nakahira. *Afterwards the* Parsee.

Enter Nakahira *precipitately, supporting* Aouda.

Aouda. Hide me! hide me—so that they can't take me away.

Nak. Aouda, Aouda! Take courage—we are in safety here.

Aouda. But the soldiers—the Brahmins who pursue us!

Nak. They have lost all trace of us, and as soon as night has fallen we shall be able to—(*turning round*). Ah, there's someone here!

The Parsee (*who has just entered* R.) I heard someone talking!—Two women—(*advancing towards* Nakahira). What are you doing here?

Nak. (*to the* Parsee). Is there any pity in your heart? Have you a soul that can be moved by misfortune?

The Par. What do you want?

Nak. I want you to save this child.

The Par. (*approaching* Aouda.) Ah! Brahma help me, it is——but 'tis—

Aouda. What, do you recognise me?

The Par. You are the widow of the Rajah, whose body is already laid out on the funeral pile in the royal necropolis.

Nak. Yes! That old man's widow, whom the fanatics want to burn along with him.

Aouda (*to the* Parsee). Oh, don't betray the rights of hospitality, but welcome the women who confide in you.

The Par. I am only a poor man, who cannot protect you.

Nak. We ask nothing of you but to give us an asylum for the night. To-morrow we will try to reach the English territory, where we shall be beyond the attacks of our enemies.

C

Original English page 25

AOUDA (*to the Indian*). No, you will not betray the unhappy girl who asks you to give her refuge. You will not give her up to those who would make her last bed amidst the flames of a funeral pile!

THE PAR. No, I will not do so——I, who like yourself, belong to the race of the Parsees.

AOUDA. Then I am saved!

THE PAR. Princess Aouda— Do what you will with your servant——he will suffer himself to be killed for you——But —how have you been able to escape?

AOUDA. Thanks to the devotion of Nakahira, the courageous Malayan, who was carried off from her country to be thrown into slavery, and who loves me like a sister—— I was married scarcely two months ago to this Rajah, whom I didn't know, and now they want me to die with him——me who have scarcely yet begun to live.

NAK. Poor Aouda!

AOUDA. For two days I was shut up in the Pagoda, where I lay waiting for the hour of torture. The Brahmins tried to intoxicate me with the "Bang," which destroys body and soul alike. I refused to take the draught. Last night, Nakahira succeeded in penetrating my retreat, and she led me away while the priests slept. The whole day we have been walking through the forest and the jungle, until we reached this dwelling, where, thank Heaven, we have met a brother and a friend.

THE PAR. The sacrifice is to be accomplished this night.

NAK. Yes—this very night.

THE PAR. Well, their sacrifice will want its victim. Aouda, I will be your guide, and I will show you the way to the English territory.

AOUDA. Thanks, brother.

NAK. And in a few hours we shall have reached Calcutta.

AOUDA. And there I shall find a beloved sister, and with her, a relative, who will not refuse to receive me.

NAK. Moreover, if your life is still in danger in India, in spite of the protection afforded by the English law, why can't you follow me to the Malay country, where I was formerly Queen and Priestess? There I should find again the mysterious divinities who obeyed my voice. Since I was carried away

Original English page 26

from my island, and sold to the Rajah, I know full well—I feel it—I am expected there—and if you will follow me, no human power can touch you.

THE PAR. Somebody is coming this way.

NAK. The Rajah's soldiers, perhaps.

THE PAR No, a man, a European.

AOUDA. Let nobody see us—let nobody even suspect our presence here.

THE PAR Come Aouda—come.

[AOUDA *and* NAKAHIRA *follow the Indian, who makes them go off* R., *through the ruined walls of the Bungalow.*

SCENE II.

FIX. *Afterwards* PASSEPARTOUT.

FIX (*entering at the back,* R.) Well, here I am——Thank Heaven, I am here first.

PASSE. (*entering at the back,* L.) Well, here I am—Thank Heaven, I am here—*(perceiving* FIX.)—No, I am here second——Dear me, is that you, Sir? We have met before at Suez.

FIX. It is true. I have come the same way as you, and I guess what has brought you here. A viaduct had given way, the train could not go on—

PASSE. And as it is necessary to take a roundabout road of thirty leagues—

FIX. You are on the look-out for some means of locomotion.

PASSE. Exactly so. In this savage country there is nothing to be found but a single cart—

FIX. Which I have taken.

PASSE. Luckily they told us of this habitation, belonging to an Indian, who owns the only elephant in the country, and my master sends me—

FIX. To hire the pachydermatous quadruped—

PASSE. Precisely.

FIX. That's exactly the object which brought me here.

PASSE. You? You are not going to try to get the elephant, I suppose?

FIX. Allow me to observe, my lad, that I was the first here, and that it is you who want to get the animal from me.

PASSE. What? do you want the elephant as well?

Fix. Yes, I do want it.

Passe. You want to harness it to your cart?

Fix. Perhaps——Why not?

Passe. I say——but what is the meaning of this? Do you mean to try to prevent my master and me from leaving here?

Fix. That's possible.

Passe. With what object, pray?

Fix. With what object? Well, I am sure you are a very honest fellow——

Passe. I am sure of that, too, Sir.

Fix. Well, I will play an open game with you. But first of all, you must swear to me not to repeat to anybody what I am going to tell you.

Passe. All right—I'll swear.

Fix. On your honour?

Passe. On my honour——but let's make haste.

Fix. (*pulling a card out of his pocket.*) Look.

Passe. Then you are——

Fix. I am——

Passe. A police constable?

Fix. Commissioned to follow up and arrest a thief who has stolen two millions from the Bank of England.

Passe. Two millions?—Ah, yes, I have heard something about that.

Fix. Well, ever since I left Suez, I have been on the track of my thief, who is going to Calcutta. My object is to delay his journey, be it only for a few days, to give me time to get the warrant of arrest, which I have asked them to send me from London——And if you will help me, my lad, you shall have ten thousand francs.

Passe. If I help you—but how?

Fix. By telling me first of all what your master is doing at this moment.

Passe. My master at this moment is performing a surgical operation on a certain Archibald Corsican.

Fix. An operation?

Passe. He is letting a little blood with a sword, by way of a lancet.

Fix. What! again?

Passe. Again and again. They have made up their minds to go on at that game, until one of the two has had the other one embalmed, and I hope that the latter will be the American.

Original English page 28

Fix. And so do I.

Passe. Then you take an interest in my master?

Fix. Take an interest in him! I have two hundred thousand francs dependent upon him.

Passe. You?

Fix. And of that sum I will give you ten thousand, if you will help me to arrest him?

Passe. Arrest Mr. Phileas——

Fix. Mr. Phileas Fogg——That's to say, the Bank thief.

Passe. A thief! he, my master?——Why you are mad. Mr. Phileas Fogg is the most honest man in the world.

Fix. What do you know about that?—You don't know him—you entered his service the very day of his departure, and he started off on some idiotic excuse, without making any preparation, without luggage, taking with him an enormous sum in bank-notes—You told me so yourself. Doesn't all this give you a clue? And then the description, which exactly answers, isn't that a sufficient proof? Believe me, my dear fellow, you had better take the ten thousand francs; and don't quarrel with me about the elephant—the only means of transport that there is to reach Allahabad from here.

Passe. That's to say, that you ask me to betray and to give up a man who has placed his confidence in me, a man who pays me, who keeps me—and merely because you have got into your head the stupid idea that my master is like the description of your thief, and you offer me ten thousand francs to commit a crime and a folly! Not a bit of it! This fish won't rise at that bait.

Fix. Would you rather be suspected of being the accomplice of a thief?

Passe. *(furious).* I, a thief! He, a thief! We, thieves!

Fix. Why not?

Passe. Who, we? *(Suddenly calming down, and speaking with dignity).* I have given you my word, Sir, and I will not tell my master what you are, or what you have chosen to tell me—but, remember this, that if I find you again on my path, be it on a railway, on a boat, or in a carriage, as true as I am an honest man, I will break your head, my fine fellow.

Fix. You?

Passe. Yes, I, Jean François Passepartout, ex-acrobat, and the first athlete in France, I, who can carry 500 kilos, and who have had the honour of laying by his heels Mr. Nicolas Krés, the bull of Provence.

Fix. Well, if you are strong, I am skilful—and we'll fight.

Passe. We'll fight—

Fix. And to begin with, I'll have the elephant.

Passe. Indeed.

Fix. Even if I have to pay for the hire, the ten thousand francs which I offered you.

Passe. We'll soon see that. I can bid above you, for I have got my master's purse. (*Striking his bag.*)

Fix. Yes, the money belonging to the Bank. Well, we'll see.

Passe. We'll soon see.

Fix. Just so—and here comes our man.

SCENE III.

The Same. The Parsee.

Fix. Come here, my lad.

The Par. What do you want?

Fix. You have got an elephant?

The Par. Yes, but—

Fix. I will hire it.

Passe. No, I first.

The Par. Impossible.

Fix. A hundred francs a day.

Passe. A hundred francs and fifty centimes.

Fix. Two hundred francs.

Passe. Two hundred francs and fifty centimes.

[The Parsee *wants to interrupt them.*

Fix. Three hundred francs.

Passe. Three hundred francs and fifty centimes

[Fogg *appears at the back.*

Fix. Well, four hundred.

SCENE IV.

The Same. Fogg. Archibald.

Fogg (*coldly*). And I'll buy it.

Passe. My master!

Original English page 30

Fix. He here.

The Par. My elephant is not for sale.

Fogg. Ten thousand francs.

The Par. (*astonished*) Ten thousand francs,—but——I cannot—

Fogg. Twenty-five thousand.

Fix. Twenty-five thousand.

Passe. Bravo.

The Par. Impossible, my Lord.

Fogg. Fifty thousand francs.

Fix (*dumbfounded*). Fifty thousand francs!

Passe. (*to* Fix, *ironically*.) Do you go fifty centimes higher, my good man?

The Par. Fifty thousand francs!—What, would you give—

Fogg. Do you agree?

The Par. I do.

Fix (*aside*). That's another five thousand francs of my reward, that he steals from me.

Arch. (*who is coming from the back, with his arm bound up.*) Fifty thousand francs! Well, you are going it. You make as light of money as you do of sword-thrusts it seems. (*Showing his arm*).

Fogg (*coldly*). At your service.

Arch. (*in a rage.*) Thank you—I don't care about your money—I believe I have more than you——And as to the wounds—

Fogg (*pointing to* Archibald's *arm*). You have got more of them, too, than I have.

Arch. But I intend to give that back to you very soon.

Fogg. In Calcutta then?

Arch. (*in a rage.*) In the bottomless pit if need be.

Fogg. As you please. (*To the* Parsee). Where's the elephant?

The Par. At the Royal Necropolis, where it is to do duty to-night at the Rajah's funeral, and I can't let you have it until after the ceremony.

Fogg. At what hour will that be over?

The Par. At about two in the morning—after the unhappy widow has been burnt.

Arch. Burnt! What? A woman burnt on the funeral pile of her husband? Is that sort of thing still done?

Original English page 31

Passe. In France, when widows burn, it is with the desire to marry again.

Fogg. *(to the Parsee.)* Where is this necropolis?

The Par. Two leagues from here.

Fogg. *(calculating.)* The boat doesn't leave Calcutta for Hong Kong until the 25th October—— It will do if I reach Calcutta to-morrow night. *(To the Indian.)* Good! then at two o'clock the elephant will be here.

The Par. It shall be here.

Fix. *(aside.)* Oh, the wretch! If I could only——

Passe. I beg your pardon, Sir.

Fix. May the devil choke you. *(Exit.)*

> [At this moment, a noise is heard outside. Murmurs are heard. The country is lighted up by torches. The Rajah's soldiers and Brahmins appear. The Bungalow is surrounded.

SCENE V.

The same. A Brahmin, afterwards Aouda *and* Nakahira.

The Bra. Let all the approaches be watched.

Passe. *(aside.)* What do these fellows want?

The Bra. *(to the Parsee.)* Two women took refuge here an hour ago—— One of them is the Rajah's widow. Where is she?—— Reply?

The Par. I don't know.

The Bra. *(to the soldiers.)* Search this man's retreat. *(To the Parsee.)* Reflect that your life is at stake.

> [At this moment Aouda and Nakahira are dragged forward by the soldiers and brought before The Brahmin.

Fogg. Ah! the hapless creatures.

Passe. What!—Are they going to burn this poor girl.

The Bra. Princess Aouda!—— according to the law of Siva and of Vishnu, you must die.

Aouda. The law which condemns me is horrible and criminal——I scarcely knew this husband to whose manes you would sacrifice me—— This Rajah to whom my life was enchained. I will not die.

THE BRA. Your resistance is useless. Before to-morrow's dawn, your ashes, mingled with those of your husband, will be cold. [*she is seized by the priests.*
NAK. (*runs to succour* AOUDA.) Dear Aouda! (THE BRAHMIN *makes a sign*—NAKAHIRA *is seized.*)
THE BRA. As for you who have encouraged her flight, your punishment shall be severe! Take her away!
[*They are about to drag off* NAKAHIRA.
AOUDA. Stop!——and listen to me.
THE BRA. Speak!
AOUDA. Alas! I realize it now——I am doomed to die, and nothing can save me——but I know how well you desire to keep up the religious zeal of your people——Well, give Nakahira her freedom, ensure her return to the Malayan Islands, and instead of a victim, whom you will have to carry to the funeral pile, rendered insensible by your arts, the people shall see me walk to my doom, my head erect, and a smile upon my face.
THE BRA. Do you promise that?
AOUDA. I swear it.
THE BRA. Your wish shall be accomplished. Nakahira, you are free.
NAK. (*in* AOUDA's *arms.*) Aouda! Do not leave me——let me die at your side—let my last sigh be breathed with thine.
AOUDA. No! Return to the country in which thou wert a Queen—and there may Heaven be your guide.
FOGG (*aside*). Two brave hearts. (*The two women have been separated, and at a sign from the* BRAHMIN, *the soldiers drag the Malayan woman outside the Bungalow.*)
NAK. (*as she goes out*). Farewell, then, Aouda!—Farewell!
AOUDA. Farewell! Farewell! (*To the Brahmins*). I am ready now. (AOUDA *is carried off.*)
FOGG (*to* PASSEPARTOUT). Passepartout! Suppose we were to save that woman?
PASSE. I was thinking about that, Sir.
ARCH. (*ironically.*) Then you have some heart?
FOGG. Yes, Sir——when I have time.

Scene changes.

TABLEAU IV.

The Necropolis of the Rajas.

The Royal Necropolis of the Rajas in Bundelcund. A vast cemetery, the tombs and monuments of which reproduce all the fanciful decoration of Hindoo architecture. A few trees of the pine species grow up between the tombs. This cemetery is a sort of funebral town. The front of the stage is unoccupied, and forms a sort of square, shadowed by large trees on each side. As the curtain rises, this Necropolis is splendidly lighted by the moon. To the right rises a magnificent cenotaph, before which a funeral pile has been prepared. On the pile rests the body of the Rajah, clothed in his finest garments. The place to be occupied by his widow at his side is empty. Round the cenotaph some soldiers guard the square. Groups of Indians and Fakirs sleep or lay about, waiting for the hour of the Suttee. From time to time a dull and drawling melody is heard, during which the names of the three divinities of the Hindoo religion, Siva, Vishnu, and Brahma are repeated by the crowd.

SCENE I.

Fogg. Archibald. Passepartout.

Fogg. It is impossible to reach that poor child.

Passe. The wretches who guard her fired at us.

Arch. (*in a bad humour.*) And if the night hadn't favoured our flight, we should have paid dearly for our chivalrous expedition.

Fogg (*in a rude tone*). Then why, Sir, did you join us?

Arch. (*as above.*) Because I chose to do so.

Fogg (*as above*). When one of the soldiers threatened me, and was going to strike me, why did you interfere, and wound him?

Arch. Because I didn't wish him to kill you, Sir.

Fogg. Ah!

Passe. (*aside.*) Dear me.

Arch. Seeing that I look forward, Sir, to the pleasure of killing you myself.

Passe. Oh, that was it, was it?

Arch. But why do we stay here, now that you have done all that you could to get into the Pagoda, and to bring away the victim? Another attempt would be utterly useless.

Fogg. That's not my idea. The elephant, which the Indian is to bring me after the funeral ceremony, I can wait for here.

Arch. Here?

Fogg. Yes. We are in the necropolis in which the sacrifice is to be accomplished. There, close to those watchful guards, is prepared the funeral pile, on which the body of the Rajah already rests.

Arch. Well?

Fogg. Some more favourable opportunity may possibly offer for saving this young woman, and as I still have another hour to waste—I shall remain. (*He draws out a revolver and examines all the charges*).

Passe. (*as above.*) We shall remain.

Arch. (*as above.*) Well, be it so, we'll remain.

Fogg (*in an ill-tempered manner*). What, you too?

Arch. Yes, Sir.

Fogg. And why, pray?

Arch. (*as above.*) Because I don't choose, Sir, to let any one say that when an Englishman and an American found a woman in danger of death, it was the Englishman who saved her, whilst the American stood looking on——That's my reason.

Fogg (*getting impatient*). Then, do as you please, Sir.

Arch. (*as above.*) That's exactly what I intend to do, Sir.

Passe. Oh, there's the late Rajah, is he. I shouldn't be sorry to make his acquaintance. (*He glides under the trees* L., *picking his way with care amidst the sleepers, so as to get near the funeral pile.* Fogg *and* Archibald *withdraw on one side*).

SCENE II.

The Same. Aouda. *The Chief of the Brahmins, Soldiers, Fakirs, Soldiers, Indians, Priests, People.*

The head of a procession is seen towards the L. *A sound of instruments and of singing begins to be heard. At first are seen the Fakirs, a sort of Indian Shakers, half naked, who howl and gesticulate, and cry, "Kali! Kali! Goddess of Love and of Death." Then come the Priests, wearing mitres, and long embroidered robes. They are surrounded by men, women, and children, who utter a sort of Psalm, interrupted at regular intervals by blows of the tam-tam, and*

PRODIGE! PRODIGE!

What a marvelous accomplishment!

of cymbals. Torch-bearers light up the scene. They are followed by fanatics, tattooed with ochre, adorned with long tails, which are wound three or four times round their waist. They wear a monkey-faced mask and a mountaineer's cap, and hold in each hand a thick club. They dance, howl, and shriek. Then follow the musicians playing drum, cymbals, and long Hebrew trumpets, two yards long. Troops of bayaderes, who dance in front of and then around a car drawn by fanatics, and zebus, sort of oxen, with great humps. Now and again one of these fanatics throws himself under the wheel of the car, and is crushed by it. The car is massive, and is drawn upon four huge plain wheels, without spokes or joints. It is covered with precious stuffs, garlands, foliage, and flowers. Bayaderes are grouped on the car, some using large fans of peacock's plumes, whilst others wave about banderolles and thick tufts made with the tails of Thibet sheep. On the top of the car is Goddess Kali, goddess of love and of death. This statue has four arms, the body is painted a deep red, the eyes are haggard, the hair is braided, the tongue hangs down, the lips are died with henna and betel root. Around her neck is a necklace of death's heads, and around her waist a girdle of hands which have been cut off. She stands erect on a headless giant. The car is pulled up R. THE PARSEE is then seen at back leading elephant, which carries on its back a sort of little Pagoda, in which AOUDA reclines. Dances, songs, &c. Guards bearing naked swords at their girdles, and long pistols inlaid. AOUDA is helped down by the Brahmins. She is clothed in a tunic, embroidered with gold. When the Brahmins approach her to envelop her in a muslin veil, she at first repulses them.

THE BRA. You have promised to die without weakness, and bearing yourself proudly!

AOUDA. It is thus that I will die, since Nakahira is free. (*Taking off her bracelets, her rings, and her necklaces, and throwing them to the bayaderes, who dance about her.*) Handmaidens of Brahma! Divide these relics amongst you. (*The Bayaderes throw a veil about her,* THE BRAHMIN *leads her to the funeral pile. She ascends it and raises her eyes to Heaven.*) Almighty God! Receive my soul. (*Brahmins approach to set a light to the pile.*)

Original English page 36

FOGG (*with energy*). No! no! This shall not be. (*Every body turns round astonished.*) This odious sacrifice shall not be accomplished in the presence of an Englishman!

ARCH. No! nor in the presence of an American!

THE BRA. Strangers here!

PASSE. (*in the Rajah's clothes.*) Hold!

ALL. A miracle! A miracle!

> THE RAJAH *rises at the top of the funeral pile, draped in a robe of cloth of gold. He has taken* AOUDA *in his arms. He walks down the steps with her, and marches through the astonished crowd. The soldiers who are about to slay* FOGG *and* ARCHIBALD, *throw themselves on the ground.* THE RAJAH *stops near them.*

PASSE. It is F——Passepartout——Let's be off.

ARCH. Ah! the elephant! the elephant!

> [AOUDA *is thrown upon the elephant which the* PARSEE *leads* L. FOGG, ARCHIBALD *and* PASSEPARTOUT *jump on the top of him. At this moment cries are heard from the funeral pile to the top of which a Brahmin has mounted.*

THE BRA. Treason! Sacrilege! Here's the Rajah! That one is an imposter!

ALL. Sacrilege!——Sacrilege!——

> [*The soldiers rush towards the elephant firing pistol shots.* ARCHIBALD *and* FOGG *from the summit of this living fortress, answer by shots from their revolvers.*
> (*Tumult. A Bramin falls dead.*)

Curtain.

END OF THE FOURTH TABLEAU.

ACT II.

TABLEAU V.

A ROOM IN AN HOTEL AT CALCUTTA.

Hotel drawing-room furnished after the English style. Lateral doors. At back a large aperture, through which part of the city of Calcutta is seen. Houses built in terraces amidst aloes and palm-trees.

SCENE I.

FOGG. PASSEPARTOUT.

When the curtain rises, PASSEPARTOUT *discovered looking at the magnificent robe, embroidered in gold, and the royal head gear which he took from the* RAJAH.

PASSE. *(putting on the head gear.)* By jove! how handsome I must have looked in this robe, and in this head-dress.

FOGG. *(enters and lays down two swords on the table.)* This Mr. Corsican is certainly very obstinate.

PASSE. Have you given him another taste of your sword?——That's No. 3.

FOGG. Yes, but this time in the leg.——Where's Aouda?

PASSE. She is in her room, Sir,——She is dressing herself in European fashion. Now that we are in Calcutta amidst Europeans, she needn't go on being dressed like a Malabar widow.

FOGG. That's true.

PASSE. Ah! Sir, how right you were to take her away from those ruffians! The idea of allowing such a charming girl to be killed——Isn't she pretty.

FOGG *(assuming indifference).* I have not seen——I have not observed——

PASSE. Dear me?——And I fancied that you were looking at her with interest, when she lay asleep with her head resting on your shoulder whilst that worthy elephant was bringing us to Allahabad.

Original English page 38

Fogg. You were mistaken.

Passe. Then how touching were the thanks which she gave you when we arrived at Benares.

Fogg. I don't remember.

Passe. Oh, don't say that——And then, when we were in the railway skirting the shores of the Ganges, it seemed to me that you were sometimes much moved when you looked at that beautiful young girl.

Fogg (*losing his patience*). Enough, enough! What are you doing there?

Passe. I, Sir?——I am making up a parcel of the clothes of the late Rajah——in which I showed off——you know——

Fogg. But what is the parcel for?

Passe Well, Sir, you see, it is embroidered all over with gold and silver——so I shall send it by express train to the Rajah's heirs! I don't want to look like a thief.

Fogg (*sitting down and consulting his pocket book*). The 26th October——It is 23 days since I left London.

Passe. (*tying up the parcel—aside.*) That confounded gas-light has been burning at my expense for 23 days. That makes 552 hours' consumption of gas.

Fogg. We shall be back in England in 57 days.

Passe. Fifty-seven more days!——I beg your pardon, Sir, but we have some time to make up.

Fogg. Indeed we have. We had saved 48 hours, but we have lost them for the sake of being of use to that young woman.

Passe. (*aside.*) That's what he calls being of use——And that idiot of a policeman fancies he's a thief——Never mind, he has left us at last, and he has done well (*pointing to his hands*), for if he hadn't, he certainly would have felt these two claws——There's the parcel tied up.

Fogg. You have taken our two places in the Hong Kong boat?

Passe. Yes. The Rangoon, an excellent goer——She leaves this evening, in two hours and a half.

Fogg (*walking up and down*). Good——good——

Passe. And now for the address. (*Writing the address on the parcel.*) To Mr. Rajah, Esq., in his tomb, province of Bundelkund.

Original English page 39

SCENE II.
The same. AOUDA.

FOGG. Ah! There's Aouda!

PASSE. (*looking at* AOUDA, *aside.*) How nice she looks in her new clothes, my widow!——Only fancy that I was the husband——the late husband of that pretty woman!——

AOUDA. Ah! Mr. Fogg.

FOGG. You haven't wanted for anything, have you?—That's to say, if my orders have been properly carried out.

AOUDA. I have wanted for nothing, Mr. Fogg, nothing thank you!——After having risked your life for me——

FOGG. I! No—not at all. (*pointing to* PASSEPARTOUT) It is that fine fellow who must have the honour.

PASSE. I, Sir? Why, all I did was to disguise myself a little ——I only played a carnival trick—that's all I did.

AOUDA. I know well how much I owe you, too, my friend.

FOGG. And here we are in the city where your relative resides, in whose care I am to place you.

AOUDA. Yes.

FOGG. Do you know where he lives?

AOUDA. No!——We used to live in Bombay, before that unhappy marriage.

FOGG. And what's the name of this relative?

AOUDA. Anardill.

FOGG. At the Exchange, they will doubtless know the merchant's address——Passepartout is sharp——he will find it out——Go, Passepartout.

PASSE. I fly!——But not with any enthusiasm.

AOUDA. Why?

PASSE. Because we shall never see each other again! (*aside.*) And just fancy, if it had'nt been for me, they'd have cooked that adorable young lady. It makes my blood boil to think of it. [*Exit.*

SCENE III.
FOGG. AOUDA.

FOGG. We have come to the end of our journey——Madam——

AOUDA (*looking at him with astonishment*). Madam! Why do you speak to me in that way! Why don't you still call me Aouda?

Fogg. Why?

Aouda. Yes, why?

Fogg. Why? Aouda——Well, because——Just look at yourself——It is no longer Aouda whom I see. No, it is a young English lady, and I speak to you with the respect which I should show to one of my fellow country-women.

Aouda. But am I not still the same Aouda that you saved, although I have put on other clothes?

Fogg. I saved you?——Oh, but you know very well——

Aouda. Yes, it was you who saved me——And from what a terrible death!——Oh, Mr. Fogg, we are about to separate to day——in a few moments——never to meet again ——But I swear to you my heart will never forget you.

Fogg (*moved*). My Lady——

Aouda (*in a coaxing tone*). Dont speak to me thus——

Fogg. Madam!——

Aouda. No, no!——

Fogg. Aouda!

Aouda *(joyfully)*. That's right——To you I am always, always Aouda——And I want you whenever you think of me, if you ever do think of me——

Fogg (*forgetting himself*). Oh, don't fear, I shall think of you——(*coldly*) sometimes.

Aouda. I want you always to think of me——understand ——just as I was, when you bore me away from that horrible torture. I want you to say to yourself: "There's a woman to whom I devoted myself, and whose gratitude will end only with her life."

Fogg (*much moved*). I promise you, Aouda——Yes—— I promise you, I declare——I swear to you——Oh, if they could only see me at the Excentric Club.

Aouda (*smiling*). Nobody sees you but myself, and you can be as kind as you like.

Fogg. I am not kind——I am——I am excentric.

Aouda. I tell you that you have a very good heart.

Fogg. A heart! a heart——Everybody has got a heart ——As for me, I am——

Aouda. Excentric! I don't know what that means, Mr. Fogg, but I will defy you not to be a little touched, when you bid me farewell for ever——for ever!

Original English page 41

Fogg (*much moved, but in a br   tone.*) Farewell!——farewell——for——(*seeing* Corsican *enter.*) Oh! there's Corsican (*aside.*) For once he comes in at the nick of time.

SCENE IV.

The same. Archibald.

Enter Archibald, *limping on one leg, without seeing* Fogg *and* Aouda.

Arch. (*throwing himself into an arm-chair.*) I have had enough of this, and I have made up my mind——

Fogg. Sir!

Arch. Sir!——I beg your pardon, Madam, I didn't see you.

Aouda. Mr. Archibald.

Arch. Dear me!——But it is Aouda!——I shouldn't have recognized you, Madam, in those clothes.

Aouda. To you also, I owe a debt of gratitude——I know the part that you took——

Arch. Oh, come, it is not worth mentioning. We only exchanged a few pistol-shots with those Bundelkund monkeys It's not worth mentioning.

Aouda. Yes, yes——but before we separate——

Arch. How do you mean—separate?——Are you not going to remain in Calcutta?

Aouda. Yes.

Arch. Well, and so am I. Calcutta is a charming city, inhabited only by Englishmen, who are made up like Indians.

Fogg (*dryly*). I thought you had sworn to take me back to England!

Arch. Yes, I know—in the mummy-case, neatly fixed up in swathes and with glass eyes——That's what I meant to do, but I have given up the idea, Sir.

Fogg. Ah!—at last!

Arch. A taste of your sword in the left arm at Suez—— a second taste in the right arm at Bombay——and now a third in the leg at Calcutta——I have had enough of it! No American should stick to a silly idea. I shall look out for some other excentricity. I am very comfortable here, and here we'll remain. (*Sits down.*) And I fancy, Madam, that you will find yourself more comfortable here than in your estates at Bundelkund.

AOUDA. My estates——Yes——I was Queen there——It was my idea to be Queen——That childish ambition was my ruin.

FOGG. How was that?

AOUDA. The relative who brought us up—my sister and me—had entered into large speculations, and he ruined himself. One day he came to me and said, "You are ambitious, Aouda," (*smiling*). Ambitious at sixteen years of age! "The Rajah, who saw you at Bombay, offers to share his throne with you." I pictured to myself a young and handsome Prince—whom I should love—and who offered me a throne! I was dazzled, carried away, and a few days afterwards the guards and servants of the Rajah came to fetch me, in great pomp, from Bombay. I set out on my way——A whole nation prostrated themselves at my feet, and hailed my arrival into my estates.—I was intoxicated with joy——I reached the palace of my husband——I found the Rajah a sick old man, at death's door, to whom I was given up as the price of a shameful bargain!——A few months later he died. And those cruel Brahmins wanted to sacrifice me as his widow—me who had never been his wife.

ARCH. You had a lucky escape from them, Miss?

AOUDA (*astonished*). Miss?—

ARCH. (*bowing*.) Miss.

FOGG. And you have come to take refuge with this same unworthy relative?

AOUDA. He is the only relative whom I have left.

SCENE V.

The Same. PASSEPARTOUT. NEMEA.

FOGG. Well, Passepartout.

AOUDA. Well, my friend.

PASSE. Well, I have been to the Exchange, I found out all the information that I wanted, and I went to see Mr. Anardill.

AOUDA. Is he coming?

PASSE. He can't come.

FOGG. He can't come?

PASSE. Not just yet.

ARCH. Why not?

PASSE. Because he is dead.

FOGG AND AOUDA. Dead?

PASSE. Dead—and buried. But if I couldn't see the late honourable gentleman, I saw a young person who was anything but dead—very lively indeed.

AOUDA. Nemea! my sister!

PASSE. Exactly, and here she is, Madam.

[*Enter* NEMEA, *dressed in the European fashion.*

NEMEA. Aouda! my dear Aouda.

ARCH. Dear me! She is really a very pretty person.

AOUDA. Oh, Nemea! Nemea!—What joy to see you again!

NEMEA. Dear Aouda, who I thought was lost to me for ever, how happy I am to clasp you in my arms!

AOUDA (*pointing to* FOGG, *then to* ARCHIBALD *and* PASSEPARTOUT). My saviour!—my saviours. Thank them, Nemea—I owe my life to them.

NEMEA. Gentlemen, I have not the pleasure of knowing you yet, but you have saved my sister, and I love you already —with all my heart.

ARCH. (*aside.*) She is a very nice little thing.

PASSE. (*aside.*) And I come in for my share of those thanks.

[NEMEA *walks up to* FOGG, *and presses his hand; then to* PASSEPARTOUT, *who makes a great many ceremonious bows; then to* ARCHIBALD, *who shakes her by the hand in the American fashion.*

NEMEA. I insist upon it—I insist.

ARCH. (*aside.*) Very nice—very nice indeed.

AOUDA (*to* NEMEA). Then you are living alone here, my dear sister.

NEMEA. Yes—alone, with no protector, and beginning to be very anxious about the future.

AOUDA. But now that I am come back, we'll live happily together.

NEMEA (*with energy*). You? you think of remaining here! In a city so near independent territory——I won't allow it—I won't allow it.

AOUDA. But why not?

NEMEA. Not a month ago, a victim was taken out of this city, and carried off beyond the protection of the English laws by men in the pay of these Brahmins——they sacrificed her, and they would sacrifice you.

AOUDA. But what must I do then?
FOGG. Will you allow me to escort you both to England?
AOUDA. Take us to England?
NEMEA. There, my sister, there will be nothing to fear.
FOGG. Of course not—Pray consent, Aouda, I beseech you.
PASSE. Yes—yes—consent.
AOUDA. But we shall delay your journey, Mr. Fogg.
FOGG. Oh, no.
AOUDA. But the serious wager that you have made?
FOGG. Will not be at all imperilled. Allowance was made for unexpected accidents, and you two come under that category.
NEMEA. I accept your offer—I accept—for her as well as for myself, and there will be two hearts to love you instead of one.
ARCH. This little thing is perfectly bewitching—How strange! my leg feels better already.
FOGG. The Rangoon will soon be getting under weigh—Passepartout, engage two extra cabins for these ladies.
ARCH. (*energetically*). No—three cabins.
FOGG. What do you mean by three?
PASSE. What does he mean?
ARCH. (*walking up and down.*) My lameness has disappeared—Oh!—No, no, the lameness has gone right away—I shall go.
FOGG. You will go?
ARCH. Yes, I have had enough of Calcutta—a hateful place, in which you find nothing but Indians made up as Englishmen! But, never fear, Sir, I shall not attempt to kill you any more. I shall follow you in order to see you lose your bet, just as one of your countrymen followed a lion tamer, to see him eaten up by his own lions.
FOGG (*losing patience*). But, Sir?

SCENE VI.

The Same. FIX. A MAGISTRATE. *Two Policemen.*

FIX *is disguised as an old Brahmin. He changes his voice so that it is impossible to recognize him.*

THE MAG. Mr. Phileas Fogg?
FOGG. That's my name.

Original English page 45

THE MAG. I am the Civil Magistrate of the 3rd District, and in that capacity I require you to reply to several questions.

PASSE. (*aside*.) What's coming now?

FOGG. Speak, Sir.

THE MAG. (*to* FIX.) Come forward, Brahmin—Do you recognize this gentleman?

FIX. I do recognise him.

THE MAG. (*to* FIX.) You have sworn to tell the truth.

FIX. According to the Indian custom, I have sworn it on the tail of a sacred cow.

PASSE. By Jove! there's an oath for you.

FIX. May Brahma's punishment instantly fall upon me if I do not speak the whole truth.

THE MAG. Speak.

FIX. I accuse the gentleman who stands there before you with having on the night of the 19th and 20th of this month, wounded to death one of the priests who presided over the funeral ceremony of the Rajah, in consequence of which, I, chief of the Brahmins, require the punishment of the culprit.

PASSE. Well, and I swear by twenty-five cows' tails, I swear by the caudal appendages of an entire flock—

THE MAG. Silence! (*To* FOGG.) Do you confess that this Brahmin has spoken truly?

FOGG. Yes, your worship—But he doesn't tell you that he and his priests were about to burn a young woman alive.

FIX. Whom Brahma had sentenced.

THE MAG. (*turning towards* AOUDA.) Madam, I presume?

AOUDA. Yes, Sir—and you cannot punish the man who has saved me.

THE MAG. We must discriminate, Madam, we must discriminate. In my opinion that gentleman acted quite rightly to save you.

PASSE. I like this judge.

THE MAG. But he did wrong to kill a Brahmin.

PASSE. What do you mean by wrong?

FOGG. The Brahmin ordered the execution of a crime—a horrible sacrifice, which is not permitted by the English law—

THE MAG. We must discriminate, Sir, we must discriminate.

Original English page 46

Passe. (*aside.*) What! again?

The Mag. The English authorities have suppressed these sacrifices in the provinces which are submitted to their rule. But on Hindoo territory they respect the Hindoo religion—even its errors—and they cannot sanction the killing of a pontiff in the exercise of his functions.

Arch. (*getting into a rage.*) But this is a shame! I don't like Mr. Fogg, nay more, I am his enemy, but in the interest of justice, and not at all in his own interest, I maintain that he can't be condemned for having saved this lady at the risk of his fortune and his life.

The Mag. We must discriminate, Sir, we must discriminate.

Passe. Oh, but this fellow discriminates a great deal too much.

The Mag. I don't say that he will be condemned, but he will be tried after an enquiry, and I must put him under arrest.

Fix. (*aside.*) Very good.

Fogg. I protest, Sir. (*The Policemen step forward, and touch* Fogg *with the end of their staves.*)

The Mag. Respect the law——Phileas Fogg, you will be confined in the City Prison until it is decided that there is no case against you.

Fix. (*aside.*) And before that can be decided I shall have got my warrant.

Passe. That'll make a week's delay at least. Alas, Sir, we are quite lost.

Aouda and Nemea. Lost?

Arch. Well, he'll never get out of that.

Fogg (*to the policemen who come forward to arrest him, in a calm tone*). Let's finish this matter at once, if you please. The vessel by which I am about to start is just on the point of sailing—

Fix. What?

Arch. What expedient has he found?

The Mag. (*pulling himself up to his full height.*) But, Sir—

Fogg (*coldly.*) At what amount do you fix the bail?

All. The bail?

Arch. He has got it.

FIX (*to the* MAGISTRATE). What bail? But there can't be any bail—It is a case of sacrilege—he must be imprisoned.

THE MAG. Yes—he must be imprisoned—but the law entitles him to give bail. We must discriminate if you please, we must discriminate.

PASSE. (*chaffing* FIX.) We must discriminate, my dear Brahmin, we must discriminate. (*Pointing to the* MAGISTRATE.) He discriminates very well indeed now.

FIX. But he will forfeit his bail.

THE MAG. Yes, if it is not high——but seeing that the matter is serious, and that the risk must be in proportion to the penalty, we'll fix the bail at a hundred thousand francs.

ARCH. A hundred thousand francs?

PASSE. (*bursting into a rage.*) A hundred thousand francs! —a hundred thousand kicks!

FOGG (*coldly*). Passepartout—the bag.

FIX (*aside*). He is going to pay—the thief.

PASSE. Here's the bag, Sir, but—
  [FOGG *takes out Bank-notes to pay the amount, and places them into the hands of the* MAGISTRATE.

PASSE. (*sadly.*) By Jove, the bag is fast getting empty.

FOGG (*calmly*). You are satisfied, Sir?

THE MAG. The law is satisfied.

FOGG. I have the honour to wish you good day. Ladies, we have no time to lose.

AOUDA and NEMEA. We'll follow you, Sir.

FIX (*in a rage.*) I not only fail in arresting him, but there is another ten thousand francs that he has stolen from my reward.

ARCH. Well, that's what I call cool. If they are all as cool as he is in the Excentric Club, I must positively become a member.

PASSE. (*to* FIX.) My good Brahmin, I have the honour to wish you good day.

FIX. May Brahma and Vishnu pull out your tongue.

END OF THE FIFTH TABLEAU.

TABLEAU VI.

THE SERPENTS' GROTTO IN BORNEO.

The stage represents a cave cut out in an extraordinary way, the end of which to the R. *is lost to view. The cave is hollowed out of huge rocks, and is covered with tropical grass and shrubs. The only entrance is by an opening at the back, which looks out upon a forest.*

SCENE I.

NAKAHIRA.

At the rising of the curtain, the cave is so dark, that the walls cannot be seen. NAKAHIRA *is dressed in the splendid costume of the Queen of the Snake Charmers. The young Malayan girls who accompany her are also dressed in their festival attire.*

NAK. It is, indeed, the Holy Cave, which I see again after four years passed on the soil of India.

THE MALAYAN WOMAN. Does the Queen desire us to prepare the fire here?

NAK. Yes, and I will light it myself, that it's heat may wake the holy serpents who inhabit this cave. (*Several women execute the orders of* NAKAHIRA, *and make up* R. *a fire with the wood which they pick up.*) Again I return to this Malayan land. Thanks be to thee, powerful divinity, who has protected the slave. Blessings be upon thee, poor Aouda, whose last words broke my chains.

THE WOMAN. Nakahira, how long we have wept. What sufferings you must have undergone.

NAK. What sufferings! What humiliation! Alas!—until the day that the young princess ascended the throne.

THE WOMAN. She who made you free! Thanks to her, you have come back to us—you have returned to our shores on the very day that the Snake Charmers hold their festival.

NAK. Yes! Again have I seen the forests and the temples where formerly our Gods obeyed my voice——but will they remember it now? Will my song charm them again? Oh, come! come! let me penetrate this grotto until I reach its most mysterious depths.—Let me meditate before I wake again our sleeping divinities—Come!

　　　[NAKAHIRA *and her companions go up* R. *to the depths of the cave.*

E

SCENE II.

ARCHIBALD. PASSEPARTOUT. AOUDA. NEMEA.

PASSE. (*entering at the back.*) A grotto!—a fine grotto—By Jove—I say Mr.—Mr. Corsican!

ARCH. (*entering, followed by* AOUDA *and* NEMEA, *who are overcome with fatigue*) Come in, ladies. You and your sister must take a little rest.

AOUDA. But—

ARCH. You must—You have been walking since daylight.

PASSE. Come, ladies, we'll first of all light a fire for you, and make you a good bed—you will soon fancy yourselves at hotel.

NEMEA. My poor Aouda! how worn out you seem.

AOUDA. I confess that my strength is going away.

ARCH. A few hours sleep will make you yourself again.

PASSE. (*begins to pick up wood and leaves, and then perceives the pile which has been prepared by the women.*) Somebody has been here before us. The fire is all ready—we have nothing more to do than to light it. (*Looking for a match in his pocket.*)

AOUDA. And Mr. Phileas— where is he?

ARCH. Never fear about him—He is gone to the nearest town, so as to make sure at any price about continuing our journey.

NEMEA. I hope he may succeed.

PASSE. He is sure to succeed.

ARCH. Possibly. Thanks to his idiotic wager, we have suffered from the shipwreck which has cast us upon this coast.

NEMEA. And it is thanks to you, Mr. Archibald, that I am still alive.

AOUDA. That's true, my poor sister.

ARCH. Don't thank me, Nemea. I am so happy to have been able to save you from death, that, in truth, it is I who owe gratitude to you.

NEMEA. If it had not been for you, I should have been swallowed up by that furious sea.

ARCH. Yes, but it was ordained that I should save you. It is only the natural consequence of the feud which exists between me and Mr. Fogg.

NEMEA. I don't understand.

Original English page 50

ARCH. Nothing is so simple. We are mortal enemies. Mr. Fogg and I, and as the antipathy which separates us must come out in everything, he had to save Madam Aouda from fire, and I have had to save you from water—that's all.

PASSE. That's quite true——The ladies' apartment is ready.

NEMEA. Come, Aouda.

AOUDA. Willingly, my sister—I am dead tired.

ARCH. And now I will go and look after some means for reaching the town.

AOUDA. Then you hope that Mr. Fogg will still reach London in time?

ARCA. Oh! that's all the same to me.

PASSE. (*lighting the fire*). He'll be in time——I'll answer that. It's true we have had everything against us; the accident that happened to the engine on the Rangoon obliged us to leave it at Singapore, and we lost——

ARCH. Some twelve hours!——That's something!

PASSE. Then we hire a pilot boat to take us to Hong Kong.

NEMEA. Where, cast by a frightful tempest on——What is this place, Mr. Corsican?

ARCH. We are on the west coast of the Island of Borneo, some fifteen leagues, I think, from the town.

PASSE. And now we loose?——

ARCH. Twelve more hours, which makes another good day's delay.

PASSE. But we can make up for lost time if we reach Borneo to-night in time to catch the American boat. Once on it, my master will soon make them put on all steam—— thanks to his bag.

ARCH. That we shall see. Well, Passepartout, you had better stop here and take care of our companions until my return.

PASSE. That's it——you go——You may depend upon me, Sir. [*Exit* ARCHIBALD, *after having given one more glance at the two women who are asleep.*

PASSE. (*busies himself with keeping up the fire, and looking at the women.*) They are off now!——How pretty they look as they are asleep——They never turned a hair all

Original English page 51

through that shipwreck! (*Looking about him.*) It is very nice here in this ladies' apartment, but we must not run out of wood. I'll go and hunt up in the coal cellar.

[*Exit at the back.*

SCENE III.

AOUDA. NEMEA.

As soon as PASSEPARTOUT *is gone, a little rustling noise is heard, and several serpents are seen gliding on the roof of the cave, and gradually coming down* L. *Two of the reptiles crawl on the ground, and move towards* AOUDA *and* NEMEA, *still asleep; then from every corner of the cave, from all the crevices in the rocks, and the roof, hundreds of serpents crawl forward, swarming and hissing.*

AOUDA. (*waking.*) What did I hear! (*Rising up and uttering a suppressed cry.*) But this is a dream!——I am dreaming a horrible dream! (*Rising and walking about.*) No, no——these horrible reptiles! (*Looking at those which are crawling towards* NEMEA.) Nemea! Nemea! my sister——

NEMEA. (*waking*). Aouda! (*seeing the serpents and uttering a piercing shriek.*) Ah!

AOUDA. My sister!——(*About to approach her, two serpents rise encircling her waist, and rising up to her neck, which they coil round.*) My God! My God! Have pity on me.

NEMEA. Aouda! (*trying to approach her.*)

AOUDA. (*putting out her arm.*) No——I forbid you to approach——I forbid—you——Ah!

NEMEA. (*crying out.*) Help! Help!

[*Rushing towards the front of the Cave from the front of which several serpents are hanging. She totters and falls insensible.*

SCENE IV.

The same, ARCHIBALD, PASSEPARTOUT, *then* NAKAHIRA, *a troop of Malayan women.*

At this moment FOGG *and* PASSEPARTOUT *appear at the entrance of the Cave and perceive the serpents which close the entrance.*

AU SECOURS! AU SECOURS!

Help! Help!

ARCH. Oh! unhappy women!
 [*Both endeavour to break this barrier of reptiles, by which they are soon surrounded. The serpents which have coiled themselves around* AOUDA *make still more horrible hissing noise, and open their mouths wide when they see* ARCHIBALD *and* PASSEPARTOUT. *The other reptiles move about with increasing activity in every corner of the cave.* ARCHIBALD *and* PASSEPARTOUT *rush forward to save their companions. At this moment the scene must be pushed up to its maximum of horror, at the moment that* NAKAHIRA *appears at* R *followed by a troop of young Malayans.*

NAK. (*to the two men.*) Stop! Stop! not a word, not a gesture——None other than I can save her. (*She then begins a low chant—a sort of murmur—the chant of the snake charmers.*)

 Mysterious divinities,
 Ye who deign to submit to my laws.
 From your silent caves,
 Crawling deities! at the sound of my voice, appear.

 [*At the voice of* NAKAHIRA *the serpents stand upright, gradually leave* AOUDA *and crawl towards* NAKAHIRA *by whom they are fascinated.* NEMEA *recovers her senses, as though she had just had a horrible dream.* AOUDA *on recognizing* NAKAHIRA, *utters a shriek.* NAKAHIRA *without ceasing her chant, makes a sign to her not to speak. All the serpents stretch themselves towards her, those on the ground as well as those on the walls of the entrance to the Cave. A curtain rises from the stage towards the flies, and gradually discloses the following scene.*

END OF THE SIXTH TABLEAU.

TABLEAU VII.

THE SERPENT CHARMERS' FESTIVAL.

A magnificent Temple, strange architecture, mingled with tropical vegetation. At the rising of the curtain, songs and dances by the inhabitants and the priestesses of Malay. NAK-

AHIRA *appears, accompanied by* AOUDA *and* NEMEA, *by* CORSICAN, PASSEPARTOUT, *and the Priests and Priestesses. When they appear, the dances are interrupted.*

A MALAYAN WOMAN. Queen, everything is prepared for the departure of the strangers.

AOUDA. Farewell, dear Nakahira.

NAK. In a few hours you will reach Borneo. Aouda gave freedom to her slave—the slave has saved her beloved Aouda.

ARCH. Thanks, once more! Thanks to you to whom we owe our safety.

PASSE. Ladies, I have the honour to wish you good day.
[*Exeunt. The Queen ascends her throne. Ballet.*

END OF THE SEVENTH TABLEAU.

Original English page 54

ACT III.

TABLEAU VIII.

A TAVERN IN SAN FRANCISCO.

The interior of a Tavern, chairs, benches, tables, beer jugs, glasses with spirits. The Tavern is entirely open at the back, and exhibits to view the façade of the San Francisco Railway Station. People of every class drinking, sailors, workmen, miners, merchants, travellers. Candles and lanterns, large fire in the fire-place. It is five o'clock in the evening.

SCENE I.

Fix is disguised as an American miner, thick velvet trousers, large waistcoat, a sort of wide-brimmed hat, leather gaiters, heavy eyebrows, thick tuft of hair on the chin in the American fashion. He looks much stouter, and is not to be recognised. Seated at a table, in front of several pints of beer, and speaking in his natural voice.

Fix. He is here, the thief?—he is here in San Francisco. I reached here by one boat, he by another. He was shipwrecked at Borneo, but his shipwreck has not dealayed him forty-eight hours even. (*Walking up and down.*) I feel assured he must have spent another hundred thousand francs to have got out of the difficulty. (*Sitting down.*) And there is my warrant running after me, and yet never reaching me. (*Rising.*) Never mind, I'll fight to the very end. That scoundrel of a servant will not recognise me in this costume. Well—I'll get into the train with my thief, I'll get into his carriage, if need be, and I won't leave him any more than his shadow. (*Turning round.*) Aha, Passepartout! What does he want here? (*Withdraws on one side.*)

Original English page 55

SCENE II.
Fix. Passepartout. The Landlord.

(PASSEPARTOUT *enters at the back, he is well dressed, wears his bag hanging from his shoulder, and has half-a-dozen revolvers in his waistband. Sitting down, out of breath.*)

Passe. Ugh! I needn't have run so fast—the ticket place is not open yet.

Lan. What can I serve the gentleman?

Passe. A glass of mint julep for this gentleman.

Lan. (*to a Waiter who passes by*). Mint julep. [*Exit Waiter.*

Passe. Tell me, mine host, how long will it be before they issue the tickets at the station?

Lan. In an hour, your honour.

Passe. His Honour thanks you——Ah! you are looking at my belt.

Lan. Yes—you have a nice little collection of revolvers.

Passe. Haven't I?—As long as you travel in savage countries, you have nothing to fear, but it's quite a different thing in countries which are civilized—and as they told me that the Great Pacific Railway was not safe (*pointing to the revolvers*), all these, you see, are to take care of this. (*Pointing to the bag.*)

Fix (*aside*). Yes, yes—the bag—that is, the stolen millions.

[*Enter Waiter with tray.*

Passe. Suppose I take it a little easy. (*Takes off his travelling plaid, and puts his bag on the table, but without undoing the strap, which passes round his neck.*)

Lan. Here's the sugar, the lemon, the spear mint, the pounded ice, the water, the cognac, and the fresh pine-apple. (*Exit.*)

Passe. Thanks—this is not only very good stuff to drink, but 'tis very good fun to make. (*Begins to pour out from one glass to another the different ingredients put before him.*). I must look like a juggler who is doing his tricks.

Fix (*aside, and looking at the bag*). That's an idea—that bag—if I could only—

Passe. There—I think I have done it now.

Fix. I'll see if I can't do you—a trick of my own.

Passe. (*taking a straw.*) Now, we'll get the pipe ready!

Fix (*drawing a little nearer* Passepartout.) That money belongs to the bank—it is mine. That money once secured from Fogg——Fogg will be unable to continue his journey.

Passe. (*beginning to suck the drink through the long straw.*) Oh, these Americans! What people they are for the absorption of liquids.

Fix. There's not a moment to lose—let's try. (*He takes a long straw, and plunges it abruptly into* Passepartout's *glass.*)

Passe. Halloa, my friend!

Fix. Don't disturb yourself (*beginning to draw.*).

Passe. Thanks—Make yourself at home, my pleasant friend. Is this the sort of thing that's done in your country.

Fix (*changes his voice.*) Yes, that's the sort of thing.

Passe. (*withdrawing his glass*). The devil it is—you man of straw.

Fix. Come! between Americans.

Passe. In the first place, I am not an American.

Fix. By all the sacraments of Sacramento, you must be a Frenchman!

Passe. How do you know that?

Fix. How do I know that?—As soon as I saw the manner in which you received me, I guessed that you were. I like your nation! If I were not an American I should like to be a Frenchman.

Passe. Well, for my part, if I were not a Frenchman, I should like to be French.

Fix (*slapping him on the shoulder.*) I like you. (*Calling.*) Hey, Landlord.

Lan. Yes, Sir—yes, Sir.

Fix. Show me the colour of your cascarinette noyau.

Passe. Cascarinette noyau, what's that?

Fix. A liqueur peculiar to this country.

Lan. Directly, Sir.

Fix (*stopping him.*) Only, as we must be careful and keep our heads, you will bring us a water bottle.

Lan. (*astonished*). Water?

Fix. Yes—water. (*Aside.*) White water—white brandy. (*Aloud.*) Come, look sharp. (*Exit* Landlord.)

Passe. You seem to be afraid of drink.

Fix. I am afraid of that drink—it is too strong by itself—but mixed with water, you'll see what it is like.

Original English page 57

PASSE. *(gaily.)* I'll soon see

FIX. Ah, ah! You're jolly! Now do you know why I like Frenchmen?

PASSE. Well—because they are good fellows.

LAN. *(bringing in tray.)* Here you are, Sir. (*Withdraws.*)

FIX *(pouring out.)* Because they are good fellows, and then because I am indebted to a Frenchman for the large fortune I am going to make.

PASSE. Oh, nonsense.

FIX. Come, just try that—— (*Catching* PASSEPARTOUT *by the arm, just as he is going to drink*). No, no—not without water. Hang it all, it's too strong.

PASSE. Nonsense—do you think it is. (*Holding out his glass to* FIX, *who pours in some white brandy.*) Here's to your health (*Drinks.*)

FIX *(pretending to drink.)* Here's to yours. (*Throws away the contents of his glass.*)

PASSE. Well—you were saying?

FIX. I was saying, I knew one of your countrymen, a certain Michel Ferrier, who returned to France a millionaire.

PASSE. A millionaire?

FIX. He assured me that within a quarter of a mile of the place which he worked, in the north of Sacramento, there was still a great fortune to be made. (*Pours out.*)

PASSE. Stop a minute!—don't forget the water.

FIX. That's true.

PASSE. *(drunk.)* A good deal—a good deal of water. (*Drinks.*) But how the devil can you find the place again?

FIX. Oh, Michel Ferrier gave me a plan of the country.

PASSE. Oh, if there is a plan—

FIX. Look here, in the north of Sacramento *(pointing out on the table the position of the mountain)*, there is a little river, the sand of which is full of gold, and which runs thus—— (*He traces with his finger the direction of this river.* PASSEPARTOUT *follows the description with an eye already confused.*)

PASSE. All right, I follow—

FIX. Well, then, as you go up towards the left, you will see a great basaltic rock, which looks like a monkey's head.

PASSE. A monkey's head—Oh, I can see it in my mind's eye.

Original English page 58

Fix. If you follow on this side three hundred paces—(*approaching his hand nearer to the bag on the table*), you reach it, and there you reach it, and there you come to a nest of nuggets. (*Touches the bag.*)

Passe. (*striking the bag*). All right, that's the nest of nuggets—

Fix. You give six blows with a pickaxe—

Passe. Six blows—why—I am going to take a sixth blow now (*holding out his glass.*) Water, plenty of water. (*Drinks.*) Capital water, that is!—So you were saying—six blows with a pickaxe—

Fix. And you find a million.

Passe. A million!—with six—blows of a pickaxe!—— I say—I say, while you are there, my friend—can't you give me just three for me—just three pickaxes—three for me—three— just three blows——splendid water that is. (*Falls across the table asleep.*) Excellent, most excellent water—that.

Fix. Victory! Now to work. (*Going to open bag.*) Locked, locked! but I will soon open it. (*Opens it.*) Here's the bundle of bank notes and receipt for the sum which he deposited in London at a banker's. (*Puts them in his pocket.*) Now I'll be off. (*Stopping.*) Oh, but I'm not a thief. (*Pulling out his pocket book and writing*), " Received on account to be given back to the Bank of England. (*Tears off the receipt and puts it in the bag.*) And now, Phileas Fogg, you can try to continue your journey, and to get over all obstacles by scattering hundreds of thousands of francs—I have got hold of the money belonging to the Bank, and I will soon get hold of my thief. (*Exit.*)

SCENE III.

Passepartout. The Landlord.

Passepartout *remains for several moments with his head on the table.* The Landlord *who has come in shortly after the departure of* Fix, *approaches him.*

Land. *(looking ot him.)* His head is not too strong——(*turning round.*) But I say, where's the other one ? Gone! ——Then, this is the one who must pay for both. (*Shaking him.*) Halloo, my friend——Look here——Pull yourself together a little.

Passe. (*raising his head.*) What's the matter?

Land. To sleep after drinking, is all very well——but you have got to pay too.

Original English page 59

PASSE. *(very merry.)* Pay! Pay?——Yes—yes——pay—
LAND. Of course, since your companion is gone away.
PASSE. Gone way—— my companion, what companion? Ah! yes, Ferrier——six blows with a pick-axe.
LAND. Come, come, you have talked enough. I want my money—— Perhaps you haven't got any?
PASSE *(rising—taking hold of the bag.)* No money—— I have got no money? *(Pointing to the bag.)* Why, this a nest of nuggets——As he was saying just now, the man with the six blows of a pick-axe——You shall be paid *(putting his hand into the bag.)* You—shall be paid. *(Ringing heard.)*
LAND. Yes Sir—Yes Sir. *(Exit.)*
PASSE. You shall be *(pulling himself together suddenly.)* You shall be—You shall be—*(gradually getting sober.)* But ——but well, but——what is this?——Do I——do I dream? *(In a rage)* Am I going mad?——Nothing! nothing left! ——But this is impossible——Nothing *(finding the paper left by* FIX.*)* What is this paper—what does it mean? *(Reading)* To be returned to the Bank! Signed Fix. *(Uttering a cry.)* Oh! this man, this American, it was he who——What a miserable wretch I am! I have let him intoxicate me like a brute, and he has carried everything off, he has taken everyth'ng from me—— and I have ruined my master!——I have ruined him!—*(crying)*—I have ruined him! *(Falling down on the chair.)*

SCENE IV.

The same. ARCHIBALD.

LAND. *(to* ARCH. *who enters* L.*)* So I can let your room Sir?
ARCH. Yes, if the train starts in a quarter of an hour, and ——*(perceiving* PASSEPARTOUT*)* Passepartout? *(Going to him and touching his shoulder.)* What has happened to you?
PASSE. What has happened to me? Something which you will be glad to hear—something that will make you happy— you!——My Master is ruined.
ARCH. Ruined!
PASSE. And through me!—who have let them—here— just now——take away all the money which he had entrusted to me.
ARCH. Robbed!——What are you going to do?

PASSE. (*who has seized one of the revolvers*) Blow out my brains!
ARCH. (*stopping him.*) Mr. Fogg——
PASSE. My master!——

SCENE V.

PASSEPARTOUT, ARCHIBALD, FOGG, THE LANDLORD.

FOGG. Well, Mr. Corsican!—Still here!
ARCH. Still here, Sir!
FOGG. Now we are in America, Sir.
ARCH. It's true, we are in America, Sir.
FOGG. In your country, Sir.
ARCH. In my country.
FOGG. Where I suppose you mean to remain.
ARCH. I shall remain here if I choose.
FOGG At last! (*Turns his back to him and walks up to* PASSEPARTOUT.) Passepartout! you have done all I told you?
PASSE. All?——All you told me?——
FOGG. You have bought the arms?
ARCH. The arms!——Yes—here they are (*aside.*) And they will soon be of use to me!
FOGG. You have retained a special carriage.
PASSE. A special—a carriage——No, Sir.
FOGG. How's that?
PASSE. The ticket-offices will not be opened for——ten minutes.
FOGG. You will pay for our places direct to New York.
PASSE. Yes—yes—I will pay for them. (*aside.*) And what shall I pay them with now?
FOGG. Well! come—come along—Passepartout!
PASSE. (*much moved.*) Yes, Sir——I'll go—(*in a serious voice.*) Well! all is over now! (*Looking at* FOGG.) You have always been satisfied with me, Sir, haven't you?
FOGG (*gaily.*) Very well satisfied, my lad.
PASSE. That's well! (*with energy.*) I am going (*about to go off*)
ARCH. I say, Passepartout.
PASSE. Sir?
ARCH. You can take all the places.
PASSE. All?
FOGG (*aside.*) What's that?—What does he say? (*Walks*

F

up and down in a rage.)

ARCH. Yes, you can take mine—(*Giving him money openly*)——at the same time as the three others (*Giving him on the sly a bundle of banknotes*) for which this will pay.

PASSE. What's this?

ARCH. Go, my friend, go.

PASSE. What, Sir——you——his enemy——you——

ARCH. Come, come——You have lost the money, my lad don't lose your head as well. (*Pressing his hand*).

PASSE. (*going off*). Oh! thank you, Sir, thank you.

SCENE VI.
FOGG, ARCHIBALD.

FOGG (*placing himself before Archibald, and looking him straight in the face*) Mr. Corsican.

ARCH. (*coldly*). Mr. Fogg.

FOG. Do you find it so agreeable to travel in the company of an enemy?

ARCH. No, I don't Sir.

FOGG. With what object then do you take your ticket at the same time that we take ours?

ARCH. To take the same route that you take.

FOGG. Then, Sir, I recommend you to take to your old plan.

ARCH. What plan?

FOGG. That of taking me back to London as a mummy.

ARCH. No, I have given up that idea.

FOGG. If you continue to follow us, I shall take to duelling again.

ARCH. Come, come! I shall not fight you any more.

FOGG. You won't fight me any more?

ARCH. (*getting into a rage*) No, Sir, no!——Do you take me for a fool?——Do you suppose I have not seen that you are ten times more clever in fencing than I am?——Do you suppose I did'nt see that you were playing with me?

FOGG. I?——

ARCH. (*getting still more excited*). That you were content to touch me slightly, when you might have made a hole through me.

FOGG. Excuse me——

ARCH. (*in a rage*). Yes, Sir, yes! You have treated me with contempt, with compassion; you refused to kill me.

Your compassion and your contempt were a serious insult ——do you hear?——And as I cannot decently ask you to give me satisfaction——I beg you——

Fogg. Well?

Arch. I beg you——

Fogg. What, what?

Arch. I beg you to give me your friendship, Phileas.

Fogg. My friendship?——Come now, that's good, I've been waiting a fortnight for that word.

Arch. Really?——And you give it me?

Fogg. I give it to you with all my heart.

Arch. That's all right.

Fogg. Now let's go and look for those ladies.

Arch. Come, now there are two of us to surmount all obstacles, and to win your wager. (*Exeunt*).

Curtain.

End of Eighth Tableau.

TABLEAU IX.

A TRAIN ATTACKED ON THE PACIFIC RAILWAY.

The stage represents a vast plain coverd with snow. At the second entrance a railway, and a telegraph wire running on posts. A little behind to R. a signalman's house, with which the telegraph wires are in connection. The stage is half dark.

SCENE I.

Two Signalmen.

The two Signalmen walk up and down in the front of the stage.

1st Sig. What o'clock is it?

2nd Sig. (*pulling out his watch*). 4.10.

1st Sig. 'Twill be a quarter of an hour before the San Francisco train goes by.

2nd Sig. If there's no delay. New hordes of Pawnee Indians have been seen about the country, and they think no more of stopping a train than they would a diligence.

[*Several Pawnees begin to appear at* L, *at the back of the stage.*

1st Sig. It's cold to-day.

2nd Sig. Yes, the sun's going down.

1st Sig. Shall we go in and have a warm before the train comes by?

2nd Sig. In we go!

[*They enter the house. The Indians glide gradually towards the house, crawling on the rails. Two or three of them burst open the door. Cries are heard. Then all is quiet. The Pawnees re-appear, holding knives in their hands.*

SCENE II.

[Pawnee Chief. Pawnees.

The Chief. The train will be here soon.

A Pawnee. There are only twenty of us.

The Chief. That's true—but we shall not attack the entire train.

The Pawnee. As the chief commands.

The Chief. The travellers will be in number doubtless, but they will stop here, and when they start again, can't they leave behind the last car, which we shall have detached.

The Pawnee. Yes—and then——(*The puffing of the engine is heard.*)

The Chief. Let our mouths be closed! Let our arms be ready to act? But listen to this, and remember it well—Strike, but do not pillage! We are the avengers of our race! It is by the death of our enemies, and not by pillage, that we shall avenge the massacre of our brothers.

[*Exeunt.*

SCENE III.

Fogg. Archibald. Passepartout. Fix. Aouda. Nemea. The Guard of the train. Travellers.

The train, the noise of which has been increasing, is seen L., *The engine, of the American shape, slowly traverses the scene, and disappears* R., *with the three first cars of the train, which are filled with travellers. The train stops. The fourth car is on the stage, as well as the luggage van, which finishes the train.*

The Guard (*to the Driver.*) What is the matter?—why don't you go on?

The Driver. I daren't, danger signals are up.

The Guard. Danger signals! Pull up at the station, but cautiously.

The Driver. Never fear.

The Guard (*looking out.*) The telegraph wires cut, the posts broken! (*To the Driver.*) Is the road all clear?

The Driver. As yet.

The Guard. Signs of Indians everywhere.

A Traveller. How far are we from Omaha?

The Guard. Fifty miles. We shall be there in two hours. This is Kearney Station.

Fix (*disguised as a negro*). I am in the same train as my thief! I defy his servant to recognize me now.

Passe. (*getting out of the car*). To let them rob me like a fool!——What will my poor master say when he finds it out.

Fix (*disguised like a negro so that he cannot be recongnized—approaching* Passe. Weather very cold, my French massa.

Passe. Go to the Devil Blackamoor.

Fix. Massa not very cheerful.

Passe. No, no, Massa not at all cheerful. Good gracious why I am talking nigger now.

Arch. It seems to me I may as well stretch my legs—— After being in this train for five days——nine hundred leagues on a railway——

Passe. As for me, my feet are quite frozen and benumbed.

Fix. Massa don't want pad hoof a little with good nigger.

Passe. Pad the hoof?

Fix. Yes, to warm feet.

Passe. All right, Blackamore, let's pad away. (*They begin to stamp together*). Ah, if ever I find myself face to face with my thief——

Fix. Massa has been thieved?

Passe. Yes! (*still stamping*). And if ever I find the ruffian within reach of my hand——

Fix (*also stamping*). Or in reach of foot, my good whitey

Passe. If I ever catch him, I'll make it warm for him.

Fix. Then Massa should make it warm to-day when it is very cold. Eh! Eh! (*He laughs.* Passepartout *gives him a kick*). Ah! if you raise your hand on good nigger, I'll break Massa's head. Zizi Camboula Coum Coum Zizi Camboula. (*Gets into car again.*)

Original English page 65

Fogg (*from the door of the car*). I think, Aouda, you and your sister would do best not to get down.

Aonda (*putting her head out at the door way*). You are right Mr. Fogg. It seems to be exceedingly cold, but in this car we don't perceive it.

Nemea. Besides, I don't call this travelling We seem to be keeping quite still while the country passes before us.

Arch. That little Nemea is quite divine.

The Guard. But where are the signalmen? (*Looks into the house*). Oh! the unhappy wretches!

Arch. What is the matter?

The Guard The two poor signalmen!——

Arch. Well?

The Guard. Assassinated by the Indians?

Fogg. The Indians?

Arch. Well then we must——

The Guard. We must be off and let them know of the crime at the nearest fort. Take your seats, gentlemen, take your seats. (*The travellers of the first carriages hurry off R.*)

Arch. (*to the Guard*). But perhaps the line is cut.

The Guard. I'll get on the engine myself, Sir, and we'll go to work with as much quickness, and at the same time as much prudence as possible. Take your seats, gentlemen, take your seats.

Fogg (*to* Arcaibald). Let's hold ourselves in readiness whatever may happen.

> [Fix *has gone off* R. Fogg, Archibald *and* Passepartout *have taken their seats in the car. The stage is empty. As soon as the doors are closed the Indians begin to crawl along the foot-board of* Fogg's *car and glide along till they reach the bar which connects the car with that which precedes it. Whistles from the engine followed by the puffing of the steam. The train moves, but the car occupied by* Fogg *and the luggage van remain on the stage.*]

SCENE IV.

Fogg, Archibald, Passepartout, Aouda, Nemea, Pawnee Chiefs, Pawnies, Four Travellers, Three Railway Men.

A Pause of several minutes—ARCHIBALD *then opens the window of a door.*

ARCH. How's this?——We are not going on!
   [*The Indians utter great cries, and begin to attack the train. The doors are thrown open. FOGG, ARCHIBASD, and PASSEPARTOUT, rush out as we'l as the travellers, and the railway men.*

FOGG. The Indians!—

All. The Indians!

PASSE. Oh! the scoundrels! (*Revolvers fired by* FOGG's *friends and the Indians. Meanwhile two or three Pawnees pillage the luggage van and others surround the car.*

ARCH. Courage my friend, Fogg (*knocks an Indian down.*

FOGG. Forward! Let's free Aouda and her sister. (*They repel the Indians who surround the car. The Indians retire slowly, while others are seen crawling underneath a luggage van. They observe where the fight is going on and get down upon the line. They then open the door of the compartment in which are the two women. The Two Women cry out.*

AOUDA *and* NEMEA (*in the car.*) Help!——(*The Indians gag them and drive them off to the opposite side to where the fighting is going on. The other Indians then reappear repelling the other travellors who give way. At this moment loud whistling heard.*)

PASSE. (*while fighting.*) Ah! listen, here's the train coming back——Courage——We are saved!
   [*All the Indians disappear.*

SCENE V.

The same, less the PAWNEES *and the* TWO WOMEN. *The* GUARD *and* TRAVELLERS.

The train returns backwards on to the stage and rejoins FOGG's *car.*

PASSE. (*discharging his revolver a last time.*) Hurrah!

GUARD. (*running up.*) Oh! the scoundrels! They detached the last car——but I heard the reports.

FOGG. Let's make haste to re-assure our companions. (*Runs towards the car and utters a cry.*) Ah!——they have disappeared!

ARCH. Disappeared?
PALSE. They have been carried off.
FOGG *(to the* GUARD.) We must positively go and pursue the Indians. They cant have got far away.
ARCH. Yes, yes! We must, we must!
FOGG. Let the train wait for an hour or two.
GUARD. That's impossible. There is only one line of rails, and we must make room for the train which is coming down.
FOGG. Then telegraph——
GUARD. (*pointing to the posts cut down.*) They have cut the wires.
ARCH. But we can't leave these poor women in the hands of miserable scoundrels.
GUARD. Sir! I am answerable for the lives of my travellers. We must be off at once. Hook on the car.
[*His orders are executed*
FOGG. You go on, Sir——I remain.
ARCH. No, you go on, Fogg. A few hours delay would cause you ruin. You go, I will remain.
PASSE. And so will I, sir.
FOGG. Go away! when Aouda and her sister are in danger? of death? No no, no——let's save them——let's save them first. Didn't we pass before a fort?
GUARD. Yes, Fort Kearney; two miles from here—— Run there, gentlemen, and the soldiers will help you.
FOGG. To Fort Kearney, my friends!
ARCH. To Fort Kearney——and may Heaven help us!
Curtain.

END OF THE NINTH TABLEAU.

TABLEAU X.

THE GIANT'S STAIRCASE.

The Scene represents a wild American place called the Giant's Staircase. To the L. *natural staircase of rocks with great steps. The staircase rises along the torrent whose bed occupies the* R. *of the scene, and takes an oblique direction. Several pine trees* R. *and* L. *on the other side of the torrent which emerges from a thick forest of pines. The ground, rocks, and trees, are covered with snow, and the bed of the torrent is strewn with enormous blocks of ice. At the foot of the staircase rises a great tulip tree, the trunk of which is two feet wide and ten feet high, the branches spread out widely from the base, and those to the R. overspread the torrent. They also are white with snow. The sky is clear as in very frosty weather. The Sun is in the middle of his course. In the distance, above the tops of the trees and the summit of the giant staircase, are lofty mountains covered with snow.*

SCENE I.

FOGG, ARCHIBALD, A SERGEANT, SOLDIERS, AMERICANS.

ARCH. (*to the Sergeant.*) Whereabouts are we Sergeant?

THE SER. About eight leagues from Fort Kearney, where you came to ask for our assistance.

ARCH. Isn't this the Giants' Staircare?

THE SER. (*pointing to the scene to the* L.) This is it.

FOGG. And this is a place sometimes frequented by the Pawnees?

THE SER. Yes, Sir.

FOGG. Moreover, the marks left on the snow admit of no doubt.

THE SER. But now they begin to divide.

ARCH. What must we do then.

FOGG. We too must divide and follow them separately.

ARCH. (*to the Sergeant.*) But these wretches won't kill two women for the mere pleasure of killing them.

THE SER. (*shaking his head.*) The Pawnees have sworn an implacable hatred to the white man. They have often attacked travellers, and they have never shown mercy.

ARCH. And Passepartout, where is he?

FOGG. He is following a track and he is to join us at the Fort where we halted last night.

THE SER. And where I left the rest of my soldiers some two hundred paces from here.

FOGG. Good!—You, Archibald, you will follow the right bank of the torrent. I will reconnoitre the track in this direction. (*He ascends the staircase.*) You, Sergeant, return to the Fort, and hold yourself in readiness to come to our assistance at the first signal.

THE SER. Good! but what shall the signal be?

FOGG. A pistol shot.

ARCH. A pistol shot, that's understood.

THE SER. That's understood——when we hear a pistol shot we shall hasten to your aid.

(*Exit, Archibald along the right bank of the torrent. The Sergeant and the soldiers go off on the other side. Fogg ascends the giant staircase, stopping a moment on the summit, examines the snow, and disappears at the moment that Passepartout comes on*).

SCENE II.

PASSEPARTOUT.

I have seen nothing.——You fancy you are on a track, and all of a sudden, every trace disappears. (*He examines on every side, looking at the ground.*) But what are these foot-prints——That is not the foot-print of an Indian——Our people must have passed by here——Well, then, I must go back to the place of meeting. (*Goes towards the right bank of the torrent. At this moment a wild cry is heard. Stops.*) What's that?——(*Looking round on every side.*) Perhaps it is a rallying cry of the Indians——I must see——(*Perceiving the tulip tree which hangs over the border of the torrent at the second entrance.*) That tree——it looks over the plain on one side——Quick!——*Passepartout runs towards the tree, and by the help of the knots in the trunk, he gradually rises himself until he gets on the fork formed by the first branches. The wild cry is heard again, and nearer. Looking out.*) The Indians!——They are bringing their prisoners here!——I must run to the Fort and let them know. (*He is about to come down from the tree when the indians appear, some gliding down the giant staircase, others crossing the torrent on the blocks of ice, others entering* L.) Surrounded on every side!——Let me see, this tree is hollow——I can hide here, and once inside, I shall be able to get a peep through some hole in the bark! (*Disappears inside tree.*)

Original English page 70

SCENE III.

AOUDA, NEMEA, *Chief of the* PAWNIES, PAWNEES, *in fuller number than in the former Tableau.*

THE CHIEF. Are they all assembled——all that remain of our tribe?

FIRST PAWNEE. All.

THE CHIEF. And not one of those who were hurt in the fight has been able to follow us?

FIRST P. Not one.

THE CHIEF. (*looking at* AOUDA *and* NEMEA.) They shall soon be avenged.

AOUDA. Why drag us so far, if you have determined to kill us?

NEMEA. You see we are exhausted with the fatigue and cold.

THE CHIEF. It is here that you are to die.

AOUDA. Must your hatred have two victims?——Will you have no pity for my sister?

NEMEA (*anxiously*). No! We'll both share the same fat—If you are inflexible towards her, let us both die together.

THE CHIEF. Listen! I had a wife and children. Your people slew them. Of all my tribe, the most numerous and the most valiant, none are left but these few warriors! We are pursued, we are hunted, from the praries which the Great Spirit planted for us. The last of the Pawnees will soon fall under the balls of the invaders—And you ask for mercy?

AOUDA. Mercy for her!

NEMEA. No, no!

THE CHIEF. Your people had no pity on my last child. It was in this place that he was struck—at the hour when the shadow of this tree passed over that spot—and it is there that all those of your race who fall into our power shall perish.

AOUDA. Our race!—But we are not Americans.

NEMEA. That's true!—oh, that's true! We belong to a far-off country which was invaded like yours——

AOUDA. And our races, brothers by misfortune, should mutually help, instead of killing each other.

THE CHIEF. You both belong to the odious tribe of the pale faces, and as long as a Pawnee holds a tomahawk, your bleeding scalps shall hang from our girdles.

Original English page 71

NEMEA. There is no hope—there is no hope left!—(*Overcome they fall into each other's arms.*)

1ST PAWNEE (*to the* CHIEF.) There is a stranger approaching in this direction.

THE CHIEF. Alone?

1ST PAWNEE. Alone!

THE CHIEF (*in a low tone.*) Separate, all of you, that he may come this way without suspicion.

[*At a sign from the* CHIEF *and the* 1st PAWNEE, *the others disappear.*

AOUDA (*raising her head.*) All gone!—what does this signify?

NEMEA. It's true—all gone away!

SCENE IV.

The Same, FOGG.

FOGG *appears at the edge of the declivity, situated between the and the Giant's Staircase.*

AOUDA. What has become of them? (*Perceiving* FOGG *and uttering a cry*). Ah! Mr. FOGG.

FOGG. Aouda!—(*Comes down hastily.*)

NEMEA. Mr. Fogg—Ah! we are saved!

AOUDA. Yes—yes!——my sister!

FOGG. Both here!— both here!—(*He unties the cords fastening the hands of the two women, whilst the Pawnees reappear slowly.*)

AOUDA. Our friends are with you, are they not?

FOGG. Our friends?—they are waiting—for the signal—*He is about to discharge a pistol, when the Indians spring upon him, seize, and disarm him.*)

FOGG, AOUDA, and NEMEA. Ah!—(*An Indian lifts his hatchet, about to strike* FOGG'S *head.*)

THE CHIEF. No —not yet.

FOGG (*aside.*) One pistol shot and my companions would be here! (*Turning towards the Indians*). Is it you who are the Chief?

THE CHIEF. Yes, I am the Chief—what do you wish with me?

Original English page 72

L'ESCALIER DES GÉANTS

The Giant's Stairway

Fogg. How much gold do you want to buy the life of these two women?

The Chief. How much gold would you want to recall to life those whom your people have slain

Fogg. Then you intend to wreok your implacable hatred

The Chief. More than hatred——revenge!——and all the gold of your cursed race would not suffice to quench it!

Fogg. And you make war on women?

The Chief. War?——Oh! we know how you make war, you people. You have taught us by depriving us of our praries and our forests, by chasing us before you as though we were herds of common cattle——and you ask why Indians hate you!——You might take all from us, our arms, our harvests, our life, that is the right of war, if you struck but us alone, but you have taken from us, our land on which we were born, the land which covers the bones of our ancestors, the land which was to nourish our children!——And the sacred soil of the country lost to us is a deep wound which nothing can heal, which bleeds from age to age, which says to every new generation: Remember! remember!!

Fogg (*coldly*). When am I to die?

The Chief. Immediately! as soon as the shadow of that tree touches this spot. (*Pointing to a spot a few yards from the tree*). That spot will mark at once the place and the moment of your death.

Aouda (*to* Fogg). It is there that we are to die, because there his son was slain.

Fogg. His son you say? Good! Now all that you want to save you is a pistol shot.

Aouda. To save us?

Fogg (*approaching the* Chief). Who is to strike me?

The Chief. Myself!——with this hatchet!

Fogg (*ironically*). Oh yes, your hatchet——with which you can still gain your object——though your hand tremble.

The Chief. My hand will not tremble.

Fogg. It would tremble I tell you if the slave dared point that revolver which you have taken from me at the breast of his master!

The Chief (*coldly*). My Master?——You will soon see which of us two is the stronger.

G

Original English page 73

Fogg. I shall see that you daren't use this arm which I have used myself against your race——this arm which has but lately killed——(*looking around him*). Look! in this very place——which killed the young man who asked for mercy.

The Chief (*moved*). Here——one——of our race?

Fogg. He was little more than a child.——I am the son of a powerful chief, he said.

The Chief (*with passion*). My son! and it was you who killed him?

Fogg. Spare me, spare me, he cried!——

The Chief You lie! my son never asked for mercy!

Fogg. Your son implored my pity——

The Chief. You lie!

Fogg. He clung to my knees, the coward——

The Chief (*furious*). You lie.

Fogg. And I pointing at him that arm which you have there, I struck him with a ball in his heart, and I saw him fall down at my feet ——

The Chief. You shall die as he died. (*He points the revolver at* Fogg's *breast*).

Aouda and Nemea. Ah!

Fogg (*coldly*). Well then, fire!——Aouda, go away! go away!——Fire! Fire!——

The Chief (*aiming at him*). Here then.——(*At the moment that he is about to fire, a shot is fired from the trunk of the tree in which* Passepartout *is hidden, and before which* Fogg *stands.* The Chief *utters a cry and falls.* Nemea, Aouda, *and* Fogg *look at each other surprised. They are struck with astonishment*).

Fogg. What does this mean? (*The Pawnees have approached their* Chief, *one of them points to the wound with his finger*).

Aouda (*aside*). It seemed to me that it came from there. (*Pointing to the tree*).

First Pawnee (*taking hold of the revolver which the* Chief *still holds in his hand.* Have our enemies invisible arms? We shall soon see. (*He points the revolver at* Fogg; *a second shot from* Passepartout *lays the Indian low. All the other Indians utter cries, and retreat terrified. They are then about to rush back again on* Fogg, *when a general firing is heard,*

Original English page 74

from the soldiers who appear at the top of the Giants' staircase, on the shores of the torrent, and on the blocks of ice. They rush on, and after a fight of a few seconds, they overcome the Pawnees).

ARCH. We heard the signal, my dear Fogg.

PASSEPARTOUT (*appearing in the tree*). And the signal was given by me, Sir.

ALL. Passepartout!——

PASSEPARTOUT (*jumping down*). Passepartout, himself, at your service.

AOUDA. Ah! Mr. Fogg, you wanted him to kill you in order to save us!

FOGG No, no, not at all, I wanted to call up these brave fellows——because——(*drawing out his watch*). Because it is three o'clock already, and before six, we must get to the next station, to catch the New York train.

Curtain.

END OF TABLEAU TENTH.

ACT IV.

TABLEAU XI.

THE SALOON OF THE STEAMER HENRIETTA

The stage represents the saloon of the steamer Henrietta. To the R. the staircase which leads to the deck of the vessel. Cabin doors all round the saloon, table in the middle of the saloon through which the mizen-mast passes, seats all round. Above a skylight by means of which the saloon is lighted.

SCENE I.

FOGG, ARCHIBALD, AOUDA, NEMEA, PASSEPARTOUT, FIX.

FOGG, ARCH., AOUDA, & NEMEA *are seated round the table, and at dinner.* PASSE *waits upon them.*

FOGG (*calling*) Passepartout! Passepartout!

PASSE. (*looks very sad, wakes up from a reverie.*) Did you speak Sir?

ARCH. There we are calling you for an hour, and you stand there and don't answer.

PASSE. I hope you will forgive me Sir—I have gone clean daft.

AOUDA. Why what is the matter with you Passepartout?

ARCH. Oh, I know what it is. (*Aside*.) Poor fellow, it is the money that was stolen.

PASSE. Yes, yes—the matter is—you know what it is, Mr. Corsican——but that's not at all. What has upset me now is a frightful dream which I have had.

All. A dream!

PASSE. A frightful nightmare. All night long I have had my gas-burner in my head.

NEMEA. Your gas-burner?

ARCH. What gas-burner?

PASSE. My gas-burner, which I forgot to put out when I left London, and which ever since then has been burning, alas! at my expense. Only think, in this dream I saw the jet get longer, and the flames out of it get longer and longer. All of a sudden I hear a furious wind, and as I was stupid enough to leave the window open, I perceive the muslin curtains, filled with the wind, float over my terrible gas-burner, which sets them alight. The fire of the curtains spread to all the furniture, the furniture to the wood-work, the woodwork to the house, the house sets fire to the district, and when I woke, I found all the city of London on fire at my expense.

FOGG. Make your mind easy, Passepartout, this dream will not be realized.

PASSE. Do you think not, Sir.

FOGG. The firemen will put out the fire. There will be nothing burnt but my room.

PASSE. Yes, but at my expense, that's bad enough.

ARCH. Never mind—never mind, forget your dream. (*Aside.*). And forget all the rest as well, my lad.

PASSE. Well, be it so—we'll forget it.

[FIX, *disguised as a nigger cook, brings in the dishes, which he has taken from a pantry* R.

ARCH. Ladies, I drink to your health. You will return the compliment, I hope.

NEMEA. With pleasure, Mr. Corsican.

ARCH. With pleasure isn't at all the word, for the wine is execrable—as bad as the cooking, in fact.

PASSE. (*threatening* FIX.). This unbleached fellow cooks dishes which a hottentot wouldn't eat.

ARCH (*pushing away his plate*). Ugh! what a disgusting

Original English page 76

mess *To* Fix.) I say, Mr. Cook, what's this dreadful stuff which you have given us here.

Passe. (*pushing him.*) Come, can't you answer, Domingo?

Fix. It's rabbit, Massa.

Arch. Do you call that rabbit?

Fix. Good Kentucky rabbit.

Passe. When you put that rabbit into the saucepan, didn't it mew?

Fix. Mew?—that not cat, that real rabbit.

Passe. Not a bit of it, the rabbit is sham, but you are a real poisoner. (*Pushing him.*)

Fix. Me good cook! Me have served rich planters.

Passe. Planters?—cabbage planters.

Fix (*aside*). My cookery is far too good for these scoundrels, but—patience! I got my warrant at New York at last, and once on English soil—

Fogg (*to* Aouda). Ladies, you will excuse me if there is no comfort here on board. We are not on a Transatlantic, you know. The China, in which we were to have left New York had started the night before, and we had to make the best of this old merchant vessel, the only one which was about to start.

Arch. And the captain would scarcely take us as passengers.

Passe. There's a regular sea dog for you!—half hedgehog, half bundle of thorns; not a pleasant fellow to kiss.

Aouda. I assure you, Mr. Fogg, that we want for nothing on board the Henrietta.

Nemea. Thanks to the care of the little English servant who asked for the situation at New York, and whom you have kindly attached to our service.

Aouda. Don't be at all uneasy about us. and we shall owe a debt of gratitude to Capt. Cromarty if he lands us in good time at Liverpool.

Fogg. But Capt. Cromarty is not taking us to Liverpool.

Arch. What do you mean? But we are on the way to—

Fogg. We are on the way to Bordeaux.

All (*rising*). To Bordeaux?

Fogg. Thanks to the owner, and in spite of the bad will of the captain, who refused to take any passengers, I succeeded in getting ourselves taken on board this vessel, but I

Original English page 77

could not possibly change its destination. Now the ship was bound for Bordeaux, and she is going—to Bordeaux.

ARCH. But in that case we are lost. We only just had time enough to go direct to London.

AOUDA. How is this, Mr. Fogg?

NEMEA. Is this possible?

FOGG. All would really be lost, if we could not find some means of working upon this captain.

ARCH And you want—

FOGG I want to make this terrible sea-dog change his route, but we'll give substantial reasons. (*Striking the bag which* PASSEPARTOUT *carries.*)

PASSE. (*dumbfounded*). Oh, great Heavens.

FIX (*aside*) Yes, you had better reckon on that.

FOGG (*to* PASSEPARTOUT, *pointing to the bag*). Ah! I dare say we shall have to bleed it considerably.

ARCH. (*aside*). The Devil!

FIX (*aside.*) We shall see about that.

FOGG. Come, ladies.

  FOGG, ARCHIBALD, AOUDA, *and* NEMEA *go up on deck by staircase at back.*

SCENE II.

PASSEPARTOUT. FIX.

(PASSEPARTOUT *is overcome.* FIX *looks at him chuckling.*)

PASSE. And now it is all really over.

FIX. (*laughing ironically.*) Eh! Eh!

PASSE. What have you got to laugh at, Blackamore!

FIX. Me no laugh, massa.

PASSE. Bleed it well, he said, did he.——But it has been bled——bled to death.——There is no blood left in it. (*He opens and turns the bag inside out.*)

FIX. (*laughing.*) Eh! Eh!

PASSE. (*furious, walking up to* FIX.) What, again!

FIX. *(ironically)* No, massa——me no laugh, me sad——

PASSE. Well, there is nothing more for me to do now, but to make a hole in the sea. *(About to go back.)*

FIX. *(laughing and rubbing his hands.)* Eh! Eh! Eh!

PASSE. (*turning round and walking up to him.*) This is too much my fine fellow. *(Boxes his ear.)* There!——

Original English page 78

there is something for you.

FIX. *(furious.)* Ah!——*About to rush on* PASSEPARTOUT, *when they both stand looking straight in each others faces.* FIX *stands in front of the stage so as to show his cheek from which the blow has taken off the colour.*

PASSE. *(aside.)* The nigger's growing white—— What's the meaning of this?

FIX. *(forgetting himself.)* Ah! you shall pay dearly for this, you miserable—— *(suddenly stops).*

PASSE. *(aside.)* And he is talking white now.

FIX. *(remembering himself.)* You will pay very dearly box on ear, Mr. Passepartout.

PASSE. *(aside.)* He is trying to get into his part again!—It is possible that?——We'll see! *(aloud.)* Domingo——my little Domingo—— I was wrong.

FIX. Really.

PASSE. *(gently.)* And I apologize.

FIX. Apologize? *(turning his back to him.)* I want something more than that. *(Aloud.)* No want apology.

PASSE. You'd rather wipe this insult out would you! *(Looks round him, approaches table, from which he takes a napkin.)*

FIX. *(in the front of the stage, stamping with his foot.)* Yes, yes. *(aside.)* I will have you taken up as an accomplice.

PASSE. *(dipping the napkin into a bowl of water.)* Well, then, if you choose *(approaching* FIX *on tip too,)* we'll wipe out the insult, my friend, yes, yes, we'll wipe it out—— *(Seizing his head violently).*

FIX. *(struggling.)* Ay? What do you mean by——

PASSE. *(rubbing off the black.)* We'll wash it out thoroughly, my good fellow.

FIX. Miserable wretch.

PASSE. *(throwing away the napkin, and holding his head between his two hands, then looking him in the face.)* The Policeman!

FIX Well, yes, it is I, and what of it?

PASSE. What of it?——You will soon see, my fine fellow. *(Tips him up with his foot, throws him down, and holds him.)* Now then, my money!

FIX. *(trying to get up.)* Ah! you fancy that I am going——

Original English page 79

PASSE. *(holding a revolver to his throat.)* My money! or I'll blow out your————
FIX. You wouldn't dare.
PASSE. I will kill you as I would a dog.
FIX. Well, then be it so, I'd rather that than————
PASSE. Don't talk bosh. *(putting the pistol nearer.)* Now then, come along, suppose you give dad's money—to daddy.
FIX. *(in despair.)* And no resistance possible—— Here, then!—*(gives him some Bank notes).*
PASSE. That's not all——I want some more——
FIX. *(as above.)* Well, then, here!
PASSE. More, more!
FIX. *(sorrowfully.)* Here, then! *(gives him the remainder of the notes).*
PASSE. *(seizing them.)* That's right! Now I won't keep you any longer, sir, I have the honour to wish you good day.
FIX. We shall meet again, you thief's lackey, and thief yourself.
PASSE. *(pretending to ring.)* Lafleur, show the gentleman to the door. *(Exit* FIX.*)*
FIX. *(looking back.)* You will be hanged.

SCENE III.

PASSEPARTOUT, *afterwards* MARGARET.

PASSE. I see them again! I have got them! I hold them! I kiss them with rapture, my dear Bank notes! At last, I can press them to my heart and put them into my bag——Come, come, my dear little friend, let's put you back into your house. *(Puts them into the Bag.)*
MAR. *(entering.)* Good day, Passepartout.
PASSE. Ah!—who—what is this, what!—Margaret!
MAR. Here's my dear little Passepartout. I saw you on the quay at New York, and when I knew that you were going to embark for Europe, I got on board too, and took service with the beautiful ladies who are with you.
PASSE. But what for, merciful Heaven?
MAR To marry you.
PASSE. Ah! no, no! never, never? *(pressing the bag to his heart.)* And they say that a stroke of good luck never comes alone.

MAR. Well, that's just it. The second stroke of good luck——is me!

PASSE. Oh! thank you.

MAR. Ah! Passepartout, if you only knew how miserable it is to be separated from what you love.

PASSE. But I do know, Margaret. *(looking longingly at the bag.)* I have experienced that grief.

MAR. Ah! if you knew what grief your departure has caused me.

PASSE. *(shaking the bag.)* And if you knew what grief their departure has caused me, my dear Bank-notes.

MAR. How solitary I found it at the club when you had left it.

PASSE. *(embracing the bag.)* Just as I felt when they left me.

MAR. I wanted to say good bye to you for the last time, not fancying that you would leave so soon, but when I reached Mr. Fogg's house, it was all shut up.

PASSE. Not all shut up, alas! There was the window.

MAR. That's true, a window——with a curtain.

PASSE. A muslin curtain.

MAR. The room was lighted up.

PASSE. I should think so, indeed! My gas burner! my terrible gas burner!

MAR. That must have been forgotten——

PASSE. A fearful thing to forget, alas!

MAR. It was very dangerous, for the wind was shaking the muslin curtain——

PASSE. Just as in my dream——

MAR. So when I saw that, I fetched a pair of steps——

PASSE. What, what do you say—you fetched——?

MAR. A pair of steps.

PASSE. *(anxiously.)* What for? what for? speak, speak!

MAR. Well, I got up the steps.

PASSE. You, you——you got up——Go on, for heaven's sake, go on——Oh! do go on. *(He seizes her, as though to make her speak.)*

MAR. I climbed into the room.

PASSE. *(mad with excitement.)* You—you got in——you—got in—and their you—you——(PASSEPARTOUT *out*

Original English page 81

of breath, unable to speak, moves his fingers like a man who is turning off a tap.)

MAR. Yes.

PASSE. Click.

MAR. Click.

PASSE. Oh! my gas burner! my gas burner! my Bag and my gas burner——too much good luck to come altogether. Oh! Margaret. *(Kisses her.)*

MAR. Well, my little Passepartout.

PASSE. Sublime woman!—She turned off my tap. *(Kisses her.)*

MAR. And you will marry me?

PASSE. Yes, I will marry you, we'll marry each other——

MAR. And when,

PASSE. To-morrow, the day after to-morrow, to-day, all day long. *(Kisses her.)*

SCENE IV.

The same FOGG, *the* CAPTAIN.

PASSE. Oh Sir, I have such good news! such delight! such happiness! She has put out my bag! And I have found my gas-pipe.

FOGG. What do you mean? Margaret. That he is going to marry me, Sir.

PASSE. Well! I can't help it—— I am going to marry her. *(Both go up back).*

SCENE V.

FOGG, *the* CAPTAIN.

FOGG. Pray listen to me, Captain.

CAPTAIN. Sit down. (Fogg sits down). If you have anything to say to me Sir, be quick. I am in a hurry.

FOGG. This is what I have to say to you Captain: My companions when they embarked at New York fancied that the Henrietta would take them to Liverpool.

CAPTAIN. Well, they were wrong. The Henrietta will take them direct to Bordeaux.

FOGG *(calmly).* You see it would be very awkward for me to go Liverpool by way of Bordeaux.

CAPTAIN. It would be much more awkward for me to go to Bordeaux by way of Liverpool.

Fogg. Come, Captain Cromarty, you wont refuse to do me this favour, and to change your route.

Captain. On the contrary I intend to refuse the favour, and I don't intend to change my route.

Fogg. No, you won't.

Captain. Yes, I shall.

Fogg. You will give in with a good grace.

Captain. Never.

Fogg. Well, with a bad grace then.

Captain. Do you dare to threaten me? Do you know, Sir, that I can call my crew together, and put you in irons?

Fogg. Pray call your crew, Sir.

Captain. Halloo, everybody! Come down!

SCENE VI.

Fogg, *the* Captain, Archibald, Passepartout, Nemea, Aouda, Boatswain, Sailors. (*Everybody has come down into the saloon.*)

Captain (*pointing to Fogg*). Seize that man!

Passe. What's this?

Captain. Lock him up in his cabin. (Archibald *and* Passepartout *take up their position on each side of* Fogg, *while two sailors come forward towards him*).

Fogg. One moment!——I will submit voluntarily, Sir, if you still insist upon it, as soon as I have read this letter. (Taking letter out of his pocket).

Captain. What letter!

Fogg. All your crew have an interest in it. It was addressed to me by your shipowner himself. Listen. (Reads) "I do not recommend you, Mr. Fogg, to take your passage on board our ship the Henrietta. This vessel is old and she now makes her last voyage. Captain Cromarty has the order to sell her at the first opportunity, and to dismiss the crew with one month's salary in lieu of notice.

Captain. Well, Sir?

Fogg. Well! your vessel is to be sold——I will buy her!

Passe. Bravo! we'll buy her!

Captain. But I won't sell her.

Arch. (*aside*). Poor Fogg! he doesn't know that he has lost every thing.

Fogg. Your owner has desired you to give up the Henrietta for the price of two hundred thousand francs, and the cargo for a hundred and fifty thousand francs, making three hundred and fifty thousand francs in all. I will give you four hundred——

Captain. No.

Fogg. I will give you five hundred thousand.

Captain. No.

All. Five hundred thousand francs!

Captain. I refuse.

Arch. (*to* Fogg). But my poor friend, you must know

Passe. At five hundrrd thousand francs!—going!—going!—gone!

Arch. Are you mad?

Fogg. Moreover, instead of a month, I will pay a year's salary to all the crew.

All. Hurrah! hip! hip! hurrah! Long live Mr. Fogg.

Arch. (*to* Passepartout). But he must be prevented

Passe. Never mind, let him alone.

Fogg. Passepartout! the Bag.

Passepartout. The Bag, Sir?

Arch. Well, well, we must make the sacrifice. (*Takes off the bag which he carries on a shoulder strap*).

Passe. (*offering the Bag*). Here it is Sir.

Arch. (*offers his from the other side*). Here my friend.

Fogg (*to* Archibald). But I don't want your money.

Passe. (*cheerfully.*) We don't want your money.

Arch. (*pulling out a bundle of bank-notes which he offers to* Fogg). Yes! yes! take these and pay, my dear fellow.

Passe. (*same business*). Here Sir, here's money to pay with.

Arch. (*astonished*). What's this? What does this mean?

Passe. Bank-notes.

Arch. Then it's——

Passe. It's found.

Arch. Found! and you never told me. (*Putting money into his bag again*).

Fogg (*taking* Pastertout's *money*). Now, Captain.

Captain. I refuse I tell you. Boatswain, excuse me Captain.

Original English page 84

CAPTAIN (*in a rage*). I refuse to sell the ship to this man who has braved and insulted me.

FOGG. You are exceeding your duty, Sir.

All the sailors. Come Captain, come. (*They surround and hold him back*).

CAPTAIN (*struggling against them*). Never! I tell you that I won't——

FOGG (*taking the bank-notes and stuffing them into his pockets*). A hundred thousand francs.

CAPTAIN (*choking with rage*). Stop thief!

ARCH. Two hundred thousand francs.

FOGG. Three hundred thousand francs,

ARCH. Four hundred thousand francs.

CAPTAIN (*repeats each time*). Stop thief!

FOGG. Five hundred thousand francs!

CAPTAIN. Stop thief!

ARCH. But, thunder and lightning! you are stuffed full of bank-notes! What more do you want?

ALL. Come, Captain.

CAPTAIN. Well, be it so——the ship is yours, you scoundrel!——you have paid for her! She belongs to you from the keel to the mast head. Be it so, but I no longer command her, and we shall soon see where this devil's boat will go to without a captain.

FOGG. There is a captain, Sir.

CAPTAIN. And who may he be.

FOGG. Myself, and here's my second.

ARCH. I accept, most willingly!——What orders Captain?

FOGG. Full speed, and make for Liverpool.

ARCH. (*repeating*). Full speed, and make for Liverpool.

Scene changes.

END OF ELEVENTH TABLEAU.

NAUFRAGE DE L'«HENRIETTA»

Shipwreck of the *Henrietta*

TABLEAU VIII.

The Steamer Henrietta at Sea.

SCENE I.

The stage represents the deck of the steamer Henrietta. Across the deck is a light bridge connecting the paddle-boxes and behind the mainmast which is seen up to the spars, the shrouds are seen rigst and left from the mast to the bulwarks, behind the beam of the engine, fitted up in American style, rises and falls above the deck, further back, the top of the boilers, safety valves, the chimney and the escape-pipe, further back still the mizen mast which is seen from top to bottom, and bears the American flag. Between the engine and the boiler is a panel which gives access to the engine room. Deck is closed at the back by a poop five feet high, with two lateral staircases. In the centre, door opening on to the saloon, on the deck poop ir the wheel where the helmsman stands, from the back of the poop is hung the boat. The engine works throughout the tableau, more or less quickly according to the incidents of the piece.

Fogg, Archibald, Passepartout, Aouda, Nemea, Margaret, The Captain, The Boatswain, Sailors, Stokers.

(*When the curtain rises,* Fogg *discovered on the bridge with the* Boatswain *near him.*)

Fogg. (*on the gangwag, speaking through the trumpet.*) Hoist the sails! Come quick!——Get up the steam!

The Boats. The screw makes thirty revolutions a minute.

Fogg. And we are scarcely doing eleven knots an hour.

The Boats. That's it, Captain Fogg.

Fogg. (*speaking to the man at the wheel.*) Steer Nor' nor' East.

The Sailor. Aye, aye, Sir.

[*At this moment,* Archibald, *who has been walking up and down the deck, comes forward.*

Capt. That's it, that's quite right——You have been a sailor then.

Fogg. I know something about it, Sir.

Original English page 86

ARCH. (*to* FOGG, *who has just come down from the gangway.*) Well, friend Fogg. where are we?

FOGG. The boat's a bad goer. We ought to be in sight of Liverpool.

ARCH. And how far off are we?

FOGG. Five or six hours more.

ARCH. And to-day's the last day.

FOGG. The last day. and I must get to Liverpool before four o'clock to catch the London express.

ARCH. But, confound it, can't we increase the speed of this cursed boat.

FOGG, The furnaces are full of coal, and we are carrying all the sail which we can in this weather——Never mind! pile on! pile on the fuel!

THE BOATS. (*with embarrasment.*) But, Captain, the fact is——

FOGG. Well, what? What is the matter.

PASSE. The fact is, Sir——The sailors don't like to tell you— —you have been paying the stokers for a week so that we may get on by piling on the fuel, and at seven o'clock this morning there was no coal left.

FOGG. Well, and then?

PASSE. So as I know what you are, I took upon myself to tell them to burn all they could. There were several thousand hams in the hold——they will never be eaten, they are too well done for that.

FOGG. Well, and then?

PASSE. Then we burnt the table, the furniture, the luggage, all the boxes.

CAPT. And my box too?

PASSE. And your box too! And now there is nothing left.

All. Nothing.

FOGG. (*looking round him.*) Nothing! and I have only three hours left.

ARCH. What are you going to do?

FOGG. Well! call everybody on deck!

[AOUDA, NEMEA, MARGARET, *come down from the poop at the back.* SAILORS *emerge from the hatchways. All make a group at the foot of the mainmast.*)

My friends! we are still forty miles from Liverpool, and if I don't get there before four o'clock this afternoon, I am lost. Are you ready to obey my orders, whatever they may be?

All.   Yes, yes.

Fogg. (*to* Aouda *and* Nemea.)   And you Aouda! and you Nemea.) Will you allow me to expose you to a danger in order to make one last effort.

Aouda.   Do what you will, Mr. Fogg.

Nemea.   Do what you will.

Fogg.   Well! my friends! fetch pliers! hatchets! saws!
   [*Several* Sailors *are bring back hatchets.*

Capt.   What are you going to do?

Arca.   Bravo! I understand him! He's right! Let them break up the bulwarks, the poop, even the deck on which we stand! Let them tear down the planks to the waterline, if need be, and let them throw all this wood into the furnaces until they fill them to the mouth! Is that it, Captain?

Fogg.   Yes! that's it, my friends.

All.   Hurrah! Hurrah!
   [*They execute* Fogg's *orders, demolishing the poop and the bulwarks. They drag on the topmast and cut down the mainmast. Meanwhile the* Captain *walks up to* Fogg.

Capt.   Burn my ship!

Fogg.   Isn't it mine?

Arch.   It's ours, Sir!

Capt.   You have paid for it, and now you are going to burn it!——I begin to like that fellow, that Englishman——He's a true American——He want's to get in——He shall get in——The ship may go to the devil. (*Joins the group and uses the axe.*)

Passe. (*throwing through the pannels the loads of wood brought to him by* Margaret *and* Sailors.)   Here you are, stokers! Here's more! more! Hold fast!

Fogg. (*to the* Boatswain.)   Well?

Boats.   Well! thirty-five revolutions a minute.

Fogg.   Good! good!

Boats.   But the steam is escaping from the safety valves

Fogg.   Then stop up the valves.

Original English page 88

BOATS. We shall be blown up.
ARCH. Very well! let's be blown up.
All. To the valves! to the valves!

    [SAILORS *climb on to the top of the boiler and put heavy spars on the valves. The movement of the machine is accelerated, and the beam rises and falls at a frightful speed. At this moment an immense jet of steam and a tongue of fire burst out. Frightful explosion. The boilers burst and the pieces fly right and left. The chimney flies into fragments amidst torrents of steam. The machine stops. Part of the deck has given way, several men are knocked down*

General cry. Ah! ah!
THE BOATS. We are sinking! we are sinking! (FOGG *is on the gangway. The* CAPTAIN *joins him.*)
CAPT. Lower the boat.
FOGG. (*to the* CAPTAIN.) But, Sir——
CAPT. Danger threatens! I resume my command.
FOGG. Well then, we'll command together.
CAPT. Together! that's right.

    [*Meanwhile the* SAILORS *lower the boat at the back. The ship is gradually sinking.*)

ARCH. Fogg! the boat is ready!
FOGG. (*crying.*) On board.
CAPT. On board. (*The boat has been brought round to the side of the ship to the* R.)
FOGG. The women first of all!
CAPT. Then the crew.
BOATS. (*to the* CAPTAIN.) And you, Captain.
ARCH. (*to* FOGG.) And you, Fogg.
FOGG. We go last.
CAPT. The last! (*Presses his hand.*)

    [*The women have been put into the boat which, in consequence of the sinking of the ship, is as high as the deck, which latter is already covered by the water.*

FOGG. (*to* ARCHIBALD.) I confide them to you, Archibald.
ARCH. Rely on me.

    [*At this moment the sea reaches the bridge, and the ship sinks.* (*Long cry.*) (*A fog arises.*)
    Scene changes.

Original English page 89

TABLEAU XIII.

A Waif on tae Sea.

The fog lifts gradually, and the stage represents the open sea. Fog still hangs over back of scene. Twilight.

SCENE I.

Fix, *afterwards* Fogg, *afterwards* Passepartout.

In the middle of the sea is a mast-top, on which Fogg *stands erect.*

Fogg. A man there! This way, Sir.
       [*holding out his hand to him.*
Fix. Ah! Sir, I am very much obliged to you——Ah! Mr. Phileas Fogg! very much obliged——Where are we now?
Fogg. Two miles from the coast of England, at most.
Fix. In English waters then?
Fogg. Yes.
Fix. Then, Sir, I accomplish my mission! You are my prisoner!
Fogg. What, what——what do you say? You are mad.
Fix. Mr. Phileas Fogg! in the Queen's name, I arrest you.

 [*At this moment* Passepartout *lifts himself up to the mast-top and attacks* Fix.

Passe. In the name of the King—look here, I pitch you in.

 [*Throws him into the sea, but is dragged in by* Fix.
Fogg (*calling.*) Passepartout!—what has become of him?—Passepartout!
Passe. (*re-appearing on the surface*). Did you ring, Sir.
 [Fogg *helps* Passepartout *to get on to the mast-top. Fog disappears, and on the horizon the entrance to the river of Liverpool (the Mersey) is seen, with houses lighted up, and the lighthouse burning brightly.*

Curtain.

ACT V.

TABLEAU XIV.

A ROOM IN AN HOTEL AT LIVERPOOL.

A room in the Adelphi Hotel, Livetpool. Windows R, *Doors* L. *And at back tables and chairs.*

SCENE I.

FOGG. PASSEPARTOUT.

FOGG *is busy writing.* PASSEPARTOUT *looks very sad.*

PASSE. The explosion of that cursed boat has spoiled all. We had scarcely got off the boat which picked us up, before we rushed to the station! No train! And even if we had taken a special train we could not have arrived in time. We only had three hours left, and it takes five to reach London by express! (*Sits down.*) My poor master.

FOGG. Passepartout!

PASSE. Yes, Sir!

FOGG. What sort of a night did our two companions have?

PASSE. A bad night, Sir—they are in the deepest grief.

FOGG. Poor women! To what danger did I expose them in trying to increase the speed in that boat!

PASSE. (*aside.*) He doesn't think of himself.

FOGG. Passepartout!

PASSE. Sir?

FOGG. I hope that madman—for he must have been mad —that madman who wanted to arrest me at sea, I hope he has been saved.

PASSE. Oh! well—there's an idiot whom I don't care much about. But make your mind easy, he was saved at the same time as that brave captain.

FOGG The fatal delay expired yesterday, Sunday, at nine o'clock at night.

Passe. For want of two hours in eighty days, to lose both your fortune and—

Fogg. But not my honour—I have lost honourably, and I shall pay—Do you know Liverpool, Passepartout?

Passe. No, Sir—and I don't want to know it.

Fogg. You will be able to find out where the Post Office is?

Passe. If necessary.

Fogg. There's a letter, containing a cheque on Baring, Brothers, which will enable my fellow members in the Club to cash the amount of my wager.

Passe. Oh! misery and ill-luck!

Fogg (*offering the letter*.) Go to the Post Office without delay, and have this letter registered. I want it to reach London this very day, Monday, before nine o'clock at night. (*Smiling*.) I shall have paid within the twenty-four honrs according to rule.

Passe. Ah! Sir—

Fogg. Go, my friend, (*Calling him back*.) I want to tell you, Passepartout, that I am very well satisfied with your services. You are an honest and devoted lad—I shall not forget—Go, Passepartout, go.

Passe. You say that, Sir, as if we were going to part.

Fogg. I am ruined——and in truth—I intend—

Passe. And I, for my part Sir, I warn you that I intend to remain with you, and that I won't budge. There! [*Exit*.

SCENE II.
Fogg.

Fogg *(alone, absorbed in reflection)*. Yes! I have made up mind. Luckily, my ruin will bring about nobody else's——And then, I am alone in the world, and no one will grieve over my denth.——Aouda! some regret, some few tears, and then—forgetfulness.——Oh, thou selfish heart!—To mourn because thou leavest behind thee no suffering and no despair.

SCENE III.
Fogg.   Aouda.

Aouda (*coming forward to* Fogg.) Mr. Fogg.

Fogg *(rising)* Aouda! Ah! I'd rather not have seen you again.

Original English page 92

AOUDA (*aside.*) I was not wrong then. (*Aloud.*) Not see me again? Why, what do you mean to do?

FOGG. To go away—to set out on my travels again.

AOUDA (*incredulously*). Indeed.

FOGG. I am ruined, Aouda!—I had a million left just now, but it is the amount of the wager which I have lost, and I have sent it to my friends.

AOUDA. So that you have nothing left?

FOGG. But fifty thousand francs, of which I beg your acceptance. (*Offering her a sealed packet.*)

AOUDA. Mine? You wish me—

FOGG. It will be your dowry—a very poor dowry, Aouda I should like to offer you one twenty times better——My madness has lost it, I must think no more about that—— However little it may be, this dowry may be of use as the basis of an honest man's fortune—a man who will find his strength and courage in your love. (*Taking her hand.*) He will enrich you, my child, if he loves you as you deserve to be loved.

AOUDA. But if you give me this small amount which you have left, what will become of you?

FOGG. Oh! as for me, I shall take refuge in the bosom of a great family, where I shall want for nothing.

AOUDA (*restraining her emotion*). Ah!—I—understand.

FOGG. You accept, dont you?

AOUDA. I accept—if you promise me, if you swear to me to do what I ask you in return.

FOGG (*distrustfully*). Whatever you may ask of me—but—

AOUDA (*with animation*). Oh, fear nothing. I shall not make use of your promise to dissuade you from this distant journey——Only, as for me, whom you have twice saved, who have no relatives, who have no ties in this country, where you go—I shall go!

FOGG (*hastily*). Aouda!

AOUDA. May I go?

FOGG. Well then—I give you my word to do what you ask.

AOUDA. Good!—You are ruined, Mr. Fogg—and however little the dowry which I possess—it may, as you said, serve as a basis for the fortune of the man whom I should love—You shall be that man, Mr. Fogg—I love you!

Original English page 93

FOGG (*taking her in his arms.*) Aouda! dear Aouda!
[*At this moment a noise is heard outside. Door at back opens with violence.*]

SCENE IV.

The same PASSEPARTOUT, ARCAIBALD, NEMEA, *and* MARGARET.

(PASSEPARTOUT *is without his hat.* ARCHIBALD, *his hair standing on end, cannot speak a word*).

PASSE. Oh! Sir——Oh! Master——I—I—I——

ARCH. Oh! my dear friend——my dear Fogg——we—we——

FOGG AND AOUDA. What is the matter.

NEMEA. The matter—— the matter is that——that——oh! I can't speak——I am choking!

PASSE. We are choking, sir——to day——not Monday!

ARCA. No—it is not Monday——it is——

NEMEA. It is Sunday, Sir, it is——

ARCH., PASSE. AND NEMEA (*bawling*). It is Sunday——

FOGG. What's this?

AOUDA. Oh! what does it mean?

ARCHIBALD. It means, my friend, that we made a mistake in a day.

FOGG. Made a mistake?

AOUDA. In a day?

FOGG. But that's impossible.

ARCH. Yes, my friend, it's impossible——but it is.

PASSE. And the proof that to-day is Sunday, Sir, is that the Post-office is shut.

ARCH. And that all the shops are shut. (*Dragging him to the window.*) There, there, look for yourself.

AOUDA AND NEMEA. Yes, yes, shut!

FOGG. That's very true.

PASSE. When I got to the Post-office——it's closed, they told me, because it's Sunday. I thought that I was in a dream——and I asked the passers by, first one, then two, then ten, and they all replied: Why of course it's Sunday! it's Sunday! it's Sunday! At all events, Sir, it's Sunday.

FOGG. But how can that be, since I noted down each day as it passed.

Original English page 94

ARCH. You made a mistake.

FOGG. Oh! I know, I know——I understand——I had forgotten——Yes, going round the world in the direction of the East, the time became modified at each degree, and we have thus gained an entire day.

ARCH. That's it.

PASSE. Yes, yes, that's it, Sir——I don't understand, but that must be it.

FOGG. And, whereas, midday struck eighty times for us, it only struck seventy nine times for my friends.

PASSE. Well, then, that's it——I don't at all understand, but that's it.

ARCH. And of this day gained unconsciously, you have lost the greater part here in Liverpool, instead of starting off instantly.

AOUDA. My dear Fogg.

ARCH. But a cab is down stairs——You have got time to catch the Express for London, where you will arrive before nine o'clock at night.

AOUDA. Off with you!——off with you!

ALL. Off with you!

PASSE. Off with us!

FOGG. Oh, I knew I couldn't lose! Aouda! you shall be rich! Aouda! you shall be happy!

(*At the moment that* FOGG *is about to start, door at back opens*).

SCENE V.

The same FIX, *Policeman.*

(FIX *is dressed as a Policeman.*)

FIX. Stop!

PASSE. (*starting.*) Here Again!

FIX (*pointing to* FOGG). Seize that man.

FOGG. Me?

FIX. And that man too——his accomplice.

PASSE. Accomplice?

FOGG. Of what am I accused?

FIX. Oh! you know well enough——Of robbing the Bank of two millions.

ALL. Robbing?
ARCH. And you suspect him?
FOGG. This is a mistake, Sir, and if you arrest me you will do me an enormous injury! If I lose the Express, I am ruined!
FIX. Tell that to others! I hold an order for your arrest, and I arrest you.
(*Policemen come forward to* FOGG.)
ARCH. (*in a rage*) Come, come, you are mad! I tell you that you have lost your wits——Do you hear?
FIX. Do as I tell you.
FOGG. At all events, Sir, if you must take me——take me off now——let us go to London, and once there——
FIX. That's impossible. I telegraphed that I had you, and I am waiting for the answer, which will give me the instructions as to what I must do with you.
PASSE. Confound it!——And I didn't drown that wretch!——
FIX. Until then, Sir, you will be confined in the Liverpool Prison. (*about to carry him off.*)
ARCH. (*losing all patience.*) Well, then, since it must be——Stop——Stop——I tell you once more that Phileas Fogg is not the thief——I swear on my life, on my soul, that it was not Phileas Fogg, who robbed the Bank of two millions.
FIX (*with energy*). And what is your proof?
ARCH. My proof! Well, then, my proof is that I did it myself.
ALL. You!——He?——
ARCH. Yes!——since I have let out the truth——it was I——I, who after the theft, fled to Egypt——where you met me. It was I who hoped that by returning in Mr. Fogg's suite, and becoming a member of the Excentric Club, I might foil the Police, and live quietly in England.
FIX. Stop a bit——I remember——It is true, you told me at Suez, that on the day of the theft, you were at the Bank of England.
ARCH. That's true——I told you so.
FIX. And that you and the thief left the Bank together, after you had drawn a very large sum.

ARCH. (*throwing down his bag.*) There it is——Three times has Mr. FOGG held my life in his hands, and thrice has he spared me.——I'd rather lose my fortune and my liberty, than let him be arrested in my place.

FIX (*taking the bag and opening it.*) Yes! yes! here are my Bank-notes!——And this man has not spent a million en route.

FOGG. He!——it was he——who——(*to* FIX). But in that case I can go.

FIX. You are free.

AOUDA. Don't lose a moment.

PASSE. Drive at the Devil's own rate.

FOGG. Au revoir, Aouda! (*to* NEMEA.) Au revoir! (*Finding himself face to face with* CORSICAN.) However guilty you may be, Sir, you saved me in giving yourself up——I must not forget that——(*To the others*). Au revoir!

SCENE VI.

The same, with the exception of FOGG.

PASSE. Mr. Archibald a thief!——Who would ever have thought that.

AOUDA, (*in a low tone to* NEMEA, *who has not ceased looking at* ARCHIBALD. My poor NEMEA.

NEMEA (*aloud*). Why do you pity me?

AOUDA. But I thought——I fancied I saw——that you

NEMEA (*with dignity*). Don't fear my sister, the heart of Nemea can only be touched by a man who is worthy of her esteem.

FIX (*showing the handcuffs to* ARCHIBALD). You will allow me.

ARCH. One moment, Sir, and I am at your service. (*Going up to* NEMEA). Do you forgive me for having dared to raise my eyes to you?

[NEMEA (*without replying falls on a chair next to the table, looks around her, seizes a pen and begins to write.*]

ARCH. Not even a word?——Never mind, it's only right.

NEMEA (*gives him the piece of paper folded up on which she*

has just written. ARCHIBALD *is about to open it*). No, not now Sir, you will read that when you will be far away from me.

ARCH. (*placing the letter against his heart*). Be it so.—— You shall be obeyed). (*Raising his head and offering his hands to* FIX). I am ready, Sir!

FIX Then we'll go. (*About to fasten on the handcuffs*). [*Enter a Policeman holding a Telegram which he gives to* FIX].

POLICEMAN. A telegram from the Metropolitan Office for Mr. Fix.

FIX. A telegram, Ah! (*to* ARCHIBALD). Here are the instructions about you which I was expecting from London. " Stop all proceedings immediately." What is the meaning of this?

AOUDA and PASSEPARTOUT. What!

FIX. Thief had never left London, was arrested a week ago.

AOUDA and PASSE. Arrested!

AOUDA (*to* FIX). But go on Sir.

PASSE. Do go on.

FIX (*dumfounded, reading*). The thief was arrested a week ago, and the money has been given back to the bank.

ARCH. (*to* FIX) Would you have the kindness to give me back mine.

FIX. Oh! my dear bank-notes.

PASSE. (*to* ARCHIBALD). But in that case, Sir, it was not you who——

FIX. But why Sir did you tell us——

ARCH. To make you leave go of my friend.

FIX (*giving him back the Bag*). I am ruined. There is nothing left for me but to resign.

ARCH. (*going up to* NEMEA). And you NEMEA, have you nothing to say to me?

NEMEA. I.

ARCH. After what you have just learnt?

NEMEA. But I have learnt nothing.

ARCH. What do you mean?

AOUDA and PASSE. What does she say?

NEMEA. At least I have nothing to add to what I wrote to ou.

ARCH. (*astonished.* What—you——(*opens the paper*).
NEMEA. Read, Sir, read.
ARCH. (*reading*). Yours is a noble heart, and mine has understood your generous falsehood. Ah! Nemea! my dear Nemea!
AOUDA (*to* NEMEA). But how did you know that he accused himself falsely?
NEMEA (*simply*). I loved him still.
MARGARET. That's very pretty.
PASSE. And my master——how happy he will be to know——
AOUDA. Why can't we rejoin him soon enough to be witnesses of his triumph?
ARCH. We can.
ALL. How?
ARCH. He took the Southern Line. We'll take the Northern.
PASSE. But the train is gone.
ARCH. Well! we'll have another one put on for us. For once, I'll imitate the example of Phileas Fogg. (*Exeunt*).
(*Scene changes.*)

TABLEAU XV.

A FETE AT THE EXCENTRIC CLUB.

In London at the new Club House of the Excentric Club. Strange architecture set off by exotic negation. Splendidly illuminated. At the rising of the curtain the clock points to half-past eight. The finger gradually progresses to nine o'clock.

SCENE I.

FLANAGAN, STUART, RALPH, SULLIVAN. (*At the rising of the curtain the fete is at its height*).
FLAN. This fête is charming.
STUART. It will have cost us the million which we shall have won. In half an hour we shall have no cause for regret.
RALPH. You would'nt fancy yourself in London here, but in the finest country in the world. Who could imagine that Westminster Palace is a few paces off, and that close by the

Thames flows in the midst of its everlasting fog.

FLAN. Poor Fogg!

STUART (*pointing to the clock which points to 20 minutes to 9*). Gentlemen in ten minutes the time stipulated upon by Phileas Fogg will be up. When the last stroke of nine is heard, the million will be ours.

SUL. At what time does the last train from Liverpool get in?

STUART. At 7.23, and the next train doesn't get in till ten minutes past midnight. So that if Phileas Fogg had taken the train which gets in at 7.23 he would already have been here.

RALF. That's clear.

SUL. Besides, you will observe that we have had no news of our colleague since he left London, that is to say for eighty days—the eighty days that will be up in twelve minutes, and yet he has met with plenty of telegraphic wires on his route.

STUART. Oh! he is lost, gentlemen, he is lost a hundred times over. Moreover, the China, the only steamer from New York which he could have taken in time to be here came in as you know yesterday. Now here's the list of the passengers in the Shipping Gazette, and the name of Phileas Fogg is not among them.

FLAN. Seven minutes more.

RAL. Reckoning the chances in the most favourable light our colleague could scarcely be in America yet, and I estimate that there will be a delay of at least twenty days in the date he fixed upon.

STUART. Only three minutes more gentlemen. (*Dancing continued. Members of the Club walk up and down. The finger of the dial gradually advances*).

A SERVANT. There are some people down stairs who want to speak to Mr. Phileas Fogg,

ALL. So Phileas Fogg.

SUL. What is the meaning of this?

RAL. But they must suppose that Fogg.

STUART. Bring them in——we shall soon find out.

[*Servant makes a sign. Enter* ARCHIBALD *and* PASSEPARTONT, *afterwards* AOUDA, NEMEA, *and* MARGARET, *who keep in the back ground.*]

SCENE II.

The Same. ARCHIBALD. PASSEPARTOUT. AOUDA. NEMEA, MARGARET.

ARCH. (*in an excited manner*) Phileas Fogg! where is he! where is he?
STUART. It is really Phileas Fogg whom you want to see?
PASSE. Certainly.
SUL. He is in London, then?
ARCH. Yes, he ought to be here.
SUL. He hasn't shown up.
All. What do you mean?
PASSE. (*looking at the clock*). And only a minute left.
ARCH. But some accident must have happened then to his train?
PASSE. He is lost.
STUART. Nine o'clock! (*Nine o'clock begins to strike.*)
ARCH. Oh! the unfortunate fellow! If he had only waited for us. Our train must have got in before his.
AOUDA. He is lost. (*Calling.*) Mr. Fogg.

[*At the seventh stroke of the clock, the groups at the back open up and separate. At the eighth* FOGG *appears dressed like a perfect gentleman, and just buttoning his glove.*

SCENE III.

The Same. FOGG.

AOUDA (*uttering a cry*). Himself!
All. Himself!
FOGG (*quietly.*) Here I am, gentlemen.
NEMEA. But why this new delay?
FOGG. I had my frock coat on, and I hadn't any gloves.
All. Hurrah! hurrah! hurrah! for Phileas Fogg.
STUART. You have won, my dear Fogg.
All. And won well!
ARCH. Yes, won well—honour—money—
FOGG (*offering his hand to* AOUDA.) And happiness.
PASSE. Ah!
FOGG (*observing* ARCHIBALD.) But, I say, how does it come that you—
ARCH. No more a thief than you, my dear Phileas, and

the proof is that here's my wife. *(Offering his hand to* NEMEA, *who takes it.)*
PASSE. *(taking* MARGARET'S *hand.)* And here's mine.
MARG. A gentle and faithful wife.
PASSE. And faithful—then I am a member of the Excentric Club.

Curtain. End.

PRINTED BY W. BRETTELL, JUN., 336A, OXFORD STREET, W.

Original English page 102

Afterword

THE MERIDIANS AND THE CALENDAR
by Jules Verne

Translated and Annotated
by Jean-Louis Trudel

This article, "Les méridiens et le calendrier," was first given as an address by Jules Verne as a follow-up to the interest generated by the publication of his novel, *Around the World in Eighty Days*. Two members of the Société de Géographie in Paris, Messrs. Hourier and Faraguet, wished to know across which meridian the date changes in the civil calendar, and Verne's speech was given as an answer to their question to a meeting of the Société in Paris on April 4, 1873. Despite the countless publications of the novel in English, this explanation by Verne of the book's surprise ending has never appeared before in translation.

Gentlemen,

The Central Committee of the Société de géographie requested that I respond to a rather interesting query simultaneously submitted by Mr. Hourier, a civil engineer, and Mr. Faraguet, chief engineer for bridges and roads in the Lot-et-Garonne.

I am of the view that only happenstance connects these letters to the resolution of the book called *Around the World in Eighty Days*, which I published three months ago; however, to set out the conundrum in full, I beg your permission to quote from the concluding lines of that work.

What concerns us is a rather peculiar situation—used by Edgar Poe in his short story called "Three Sundays in a Week"—the very situation, I should say, attending travellers who complete a trip around the world, whether heading east or west. In the first case, they will have gained a day; in the second, they will have lost it—when they come back to their point of departure.

Indeed, as I put it in my book:

"In journeying eastward he [Phileas Fogg, the novel's hero] had gone towards the sun, and the days therefore diminished for him as many times four minutes as he crossed degrees in this direction. There are three hundred and sixty degrees on the circumference of the earth; and these three hundred and sixty degrees, multiplied by four minutes, gives precisely twenty-four hours—that is, the day unconsciously gained. In other words, while Phileas Fogg, going eastward, saw the sun pass the meridian *eighty* times, his friends in London only saw it pass the meridian *seventy-nine* times. This is why they awaited him at the Reform Club on Saturday, and not Sunday, as Mr. Fogg thought."[1]

That is the question at issue, and it may be outlined in a few words.

Any time that we circle the globe by travelling eastward, we gain a day. Any time that we circle the globe by travelling westward, we lose a day—that is, the 24 hours that the Sun's apparent motion requires for it to go around the entire Earth—and this occurs however long it takes to complete the journey.

This result is real enough that our navy's administration grants one more day's worth of rations to the ships that set off from Europe and sail around the Cape of Good Hope, while it grants one fewer day's worth of rations to the ships that sail around Cape Horn. Which leads us to draw the rather bizarre conclusion that the sailors heading east are better fed than the ones heading west. In fact, when all of them return to their point of departure, having lived through the same number of minutes, some will have enjoyed one more breakfast, one more dinner, and one more supper than the rest. To which one might answer that the former worked one more day. Undoubtedly, though they will not have "lived" any longer.

It is therefore obvious, gentlemen, that the matter of this day lost or gained depending on the direction of travel, and, consequently, that the corresponding date change must take place in some part of the globe. But in what part? Such is the problem to be solved, and it isn't surprising that it drew the attention of the two letter-writers. These two

---

1. From the 1873 edition of the translation by George Makepeace Towle of Verne's *Le tour du monde en quatre-vingts jours*.

Afterword: The Meridians and the Calendar | 153

letters may, in short, be summarized as follows. Yes, there is a preferred meridian along which the changeover happens, asserts Mr. Faraguet. Where is this preferred meridian? asks Mr. Hourier.

First of all, gentlemen, I shall say it would be difficult to answer from a purely cosmographical standpoint. Ah, if Messrs. Hourier and Faraguet could tell me where the sun first rose on the morn of Creation, if they knew on which of the globe's meridian it was noon for the first time, the question would be easily settled and I would tell them: this original meridian is the preferred meridian determined by Mr. Faraguet and sought by Mr. Hourier. However, neither engineer is so ancient as to have seen the first sunrise; therefore, they are unable to tell me which was the first meridian, so that, setting aside for now the purely scientific question, I next tackle the practical question that I will attempt to clear up in a few words.

As a result of the fact that a day is gained by travelling eastward and lost by travelling westward, standing contradictions have endured for many years. The first navigators imposed, unwittingly, their day count in newly discovered lands. In a general way, days were counted according to whether the countries had been discovered from the east or the west. Europeans, when they reached these unknown regions inhabited by natives who did not care on which day or date they ate their fellow beings— Europeans, as I was saying, imposed their calendar and that was it. Thus, for centuries, the date in Canton went back to the arrival of Marco Polo and the date in the Philippines to the arrival of Magellan.

But the lack of agreement as to the date was bound to create difficulties for business. Therefore, less than twenty years ago, exactly when I cannot say though our learned colleague, Admiral Paris [sic], could pin it down, it was decided to impose the European calendar in Manila—which straightened out the confusion and created an official, so to speak, day of the month.[2]

I shall add that, in practice, there has long been a compensatory meridian, which was the 180th counting from the 0th meridian according to which the shipboard chronometers were set originally, which would be Greenwich for the United Kingdom, Paris for France, and Washington for the United States.

---

2. François-Edmond Pâris (1806-1893), French admiral, explorer, and historian.

Indeed, here is my translation of what I find in the English journal *Nature*, which had received in 1872 the question also posed by our two eminent engineers:

"Mr. Pearson's query, in *Nature* of Nov. 28, does not admit of any exact or scientific answer, for there is no natural line of demarcation or change, and the settlement is entirely a matter of usage or convenience. It is not very many years since the dates at Manilla [sic] and Macao were different; and till the cession of the Alaska Territory to the Americans, the date there was different from that in the British Territory adjoining. The rule now generally held is, that places in E. long. date as if they were arrived at by the Cape of Good Hope, and places in W. long[.] as if they were reached *via* Cape Horn—a rule that the width of the Pacific renders practically convenient. Afloat, the rule is for a ship making a passage to change her date on crossing the meridian of 180°, or as soon after as the captain may find convenient; repeating or omitting a day, according to the direction in which she is going; but a ship merely cruising across the meridian, with the intention of returning, does not generally change her date, so that ships having different dates may and do occasionally meet—a very marked instance of which occurred during the Russian war, when our squadron from the Pacific joined the China squadron on the coast of Kamschatka [sic]."[3]

The above quotation, gentlemen, must lead you to anticipate the possible solution that we will outline. I have now dealt with the question from a historical standpoint, then from a practical standpoint; however, has it been solved scientifically? No, though the solution is indicated in the letter from Mr. Faraguet.

Therefore, in order to solve it completely, please allow me, gentlemen, to quote from a letter addressed to me personally by one of our greatest mathematicians, Mr. J. Bertrand, of the Institut.[4]

"Our conversation yesterday gave me the idea of a problem that may be stated thus. A gentleman provided with the appropriate

---

3. Instead of translating from the French back into the original English, the text from the actual letter signed by J. K. Laughton of the Royal Naval College in the December 12th, 1872, issue of *Nature*, was used. The only significant discrepancy introduced by Verne's translation (as published) is an inexplicable modification of the date of Pearson's query.

4. Joseph Louis François Bertrand (1822-1900), an eminent mathematician who would be named by the French Academy of Sciences to the position of permanent secretary for the mathematical sciences the following year, in 1874.

means of transportation leaves Paris at noon, on a Thursday. He heads for Brest, from thence to New York, to San Francisco, Edo, etc. He returns to Paris after having travelled for 24 hours, covering 15 degrees per hour.

"Every time he stops, he asks: What time is it? Without fail, he is told that it's noon. He then asks: What day of the week is it?

"In Brest, he is told: Thursday. In New York, the same... but, upon his return, in Pontoise for instance, he is told it's Friday.[5]

"Where did the change happen? Along which meridian does our traveler, if he is a good Catholic, throw away, as he must, the ham that is now forbidden to him?

"Obviously, the transition is perforce sudden. It will happen at sea or in the lands that are unaware of the day of the week.

"However, let us suppose a parallel stretching across an entire continent along which are found civilized inhabitants speaking the same language and subject to the same laws: there will then be two neighbors separated by a hedge, one of whom will say today at noon: "It's Thursday", while the other one will say: "It's Friday".

"Let us assume, furthermore, that one lives in Sèvres and the other in Bellevue. Before eight days have passed in such a situation, they will have come to agree on the calendar. Thus, the ambiguity will cease to exist, but it will arise again elsewhere and we will have as a consequence a continuous shifting in the dictionary of the days of the week."

It seems to me that this letter, gentlemen, both very logical and very witty, resolves categorically the question submitted to the Société de géographie.

Yes, an ambiguity does exist, but it exists latently, so to speak. Yes, if a parallel did traverse the inhabited continents, the inhabitants along that parallel would disagree. However, it seems that foresighted Nature did not wish to provide humans with one more cause for disputation. She prudently separated great nation from great nation with deserts and oceans. The transition from the day gained to the day lost occurs unnoticeably across the seas that divide the world's nations, but the ambiguity cannot be observed since a ship at sea is mobile and does not reside in the middle of these deserted immensities.

I need no longer belabor the point, gentlemen, and I will summarize the preceding as follows:

---

5. Pontoise is an outlying suburb of Paris.

From a practical standpoint:

1st. Agreement as to the date was achieved by the adoption of the calendar in Manila.

2nd. Captains change the date of their logbook when they cross the 180th meridian, *i.e.* the extension of the meridian by which their chronometer was originally set.

From a scientific standpoint:

The transition happens smoothly, insensibly, either in the deserted stretches or in the middle of the oceans that separate inhabited lands.

Thus, we will be spared in the future the painful sight of two civilized peoples taking up arms and fighting for the honor of a national calendar.

Appendix

THE PLAY ON SCREEN
by Brian Taves

Today, no less than in Jules Verne's lifetime, the author is as well known for his performing arts incarnations as for his prose. In the 19th century, the recognition was for stage versions of his novels; in the 20th and 21st centuries the theatrical enactment of his stories continues—but augmented by the new medium of the screen. In the case of *Around the World in Eighty Days*, film and television versions have been viewed by even more individuals than have read the novel. Hence, in this volume of the North American Jules Verne Society's Palik series offering Verne's own theatrical version of the book, a word about those adaptations is in order, particularly since the play as well as the novel has been brought to the screen.

In the more than 135 years since the Verne-d'Ennery text was first staged, there have likely been hundreds of theatrical versions of *Around the World in Eighty Days*, and as a play it has been as enduringly popular as the novel. It is also a perennial in productions geared toward young audiences and such specialties as on-ice presentations (themselves often shown on television). In the United States, in the initial decade of the 21st century, several new stage adaptations toured the country, demonstrating their continued viability even when competing with screen adaptations.

The vitality of *Around the World in Eighty Days* has also been evident in the audio realm. Just a week before the infamous Halloween-day broadcast of *The War of the Worlds*, on October 23, 1938 the *Mercury Theater* had presented *Around the World in 80 Days* over CBS, adapted by and starring Orson Welles. In 1946, Welles created his own commercially unsuccessful stage version, with music by Cole Porter, which in turn became the basis for a half-hour radio broadcast that year on the *Mercury Summer Theater of the Air*, and reprised a few years later on *The Railroad Hour / The Gordon Macrae Show*. Around this time, the novel would also be adapted on such radio anthologies as *From the Bookshelf of the World, Hallmark Playhouse, Favorite Story*, and on the BBC. The story is as popular today in the audiobook realm, in English and in other languages.

Big screen recollections of *Around the World in Eighty Days* usually center on the 1956 spectacle produced by Michael Todd, the climax of a show-business career that had also included involvement with the Welles-Porter theatrical presentation. Todd's film was the first true movie version of the novel, and it was echoed on television in *The Phil Silvers Show: Sgt. Bilko Goes Around the World* (1957) and the documentaries *Round the World in 90 Minutes* (1957) and *Around the World of Michael Todd* (1968). The movie also led to a 1962 stage incarnation as a musical, by Sammy Fain, Victor Young, Sig Herzig, and Harold Adamson. Budding filmmakers were also inspired, including 12-year-old Nicholas Meyer, who shot his own feature-length home movie version on 8 mm., before he became a successful novelist, screenwriter, and director.

The Todd movie was influential in defining the expectations for other Vernian cinematic presentations, and has remained vastly superior to other big-screen productions of the book. This was particularly true of the 2004 version that transformed Aouda into a French lass, rather than have two Asian leads, since Passepartout was to be played by Jackie Chan. However, television renderings have been worthwhile, most notably the 1989 six-hour television mini-series in the United States with Pierce Brosnan ideally cast in the lead role. (This version included the play's end on a triple wedding, but that was the only incident in common, likely an accidental one.)

The novel had also appeared frequently on the European small screen, with an adaptation broadcast in West Germany in 1964. In France, the story was presented as a two-hour telefilm in 1979, and as a six part television miniseries combining live action and animation over the holiday season from 1980-1981. A 1961 Czech communist parody of the story by Pavel Kohout, mocking capitalism, England's colonialism and class system, American racism, and the Vernian style generally, appeared on East German television in 1963, and the following year on Czech television, broadcast direct from a stage presentation. A 1979 stage version of the Kohout play for Comédie des Champs-Élysées was shown on French television featuring three actors from the play.

A major animated tradition of presenting the story also developed, one that exceeded in frequency the live-action television versions, and rivaled them in quality. *Festival of Family Classics* offered the story in 1972, and that same year, from Australia, came a series of sixteen half-hour episodes, adapting the novel. A new way of presenting the novel, with animals portraying the characters, was pioneered in the 1981 Spanish produced series of 26 half-hour episodes, *La Vuelta al Mundo de Willy Fogg / Around the World With Willy Fogg*, and the same approach was followed in a 1988 Burbank Films production entitled *Around the World in 80 Days*. A 2000 French version with Simon Callow as Fogg returned to the more traditional animated form. There have also been many segments of animated series integrating ideas from the novel into the series format, such as a 1996 episode of *Pinky and the Brain*, "Around the World in 80 Narfs."

The very first movie of the novel, back in 1913, operated simultaneously as a parody and an adaptation. The German *Die Jagd Nach der Hundertpfunnote Oder die Reise Um die Welt* (*The Hunt for the Hundred Pound Note or the Trip Around the World*) was released in the United States as *Chasing a Million, Or, Round the World in 80 Days*. Losing money at the Reform Club, a man receives a promising offer to inherit a California gold mine that requires he make the round the world journey in 80 days from his club in Edinburgh, and return a 100 pound note already in circulation. The same year—1913—an Italian film, *Le Aventure di Saturnino Farandola: Farandola Contro Fileas-Fogg*, was based on a portion of Albert Robida's epic 1879 novel, *Voyages très extraordinaires de Saturnin Farandoul dans les cinq ou six parties du monde et dans touts les pays connus et même inconnus de M. Jules Verne* (*Very Extraordinary Journeys of Saturnin Farandoul in the Five or Six Parts of the World and in All the Known and Unknown Countries of Mr. Jules Verne*), which includes Captain Nemo, Phileas Fogg, and many other Verne characters. Pastiches of Verne dated from Robida, a vein that filmmakers would partake of, including additional races around the world by Phileas Fogg's descendants. There were also

"Phileades," individuals who actually try to replicate Fogg's fictional trip, from Nellie Bly in the 1880s to Michael Palin a century later.

Sequels had always been an important part of the Verne canon, since the author himself made use of this concept when, at the outset of his career, he started producing sequels to his own work, from *Autour de la lune* (*Around the Moon*, 1869) and *Sans dessus dessous* (*Topsy-turvy*, 1889), to *L'Île mystérieuse* (*The Mysterious Island*, 1874) and *Maître du monde* (*Master of the World*, 1904). His play, *Journey Through the Impossible*, both lampooned and provided further exploits and situations from many of his novels. He would also author original sequels to two novels by other writers that had influenced him: *Seconde patrie* (*Second Homeland*, 1900), another adventure of Johann Wyss's family of the Swiss Robinson, and *Le Sphinx des glaces* (*The Sphinx of the Ice*, 1897) wound up Edgar Allan Poe's *The Narrative of Arthur Gordon Pym of Nantucket* (1838).

Following the first German and Italian movies of Fogg's journey, the initial American production of *Around the World in Eighty Days* was updated to contemporary times. The 1922-1923 Universal serial, *Around the World in 18 Days*, used all the latest inventions, from airplanes to speedboats and submarines, in the global trek of Phileas Fogg, Jr. The same year, a major stage pastiche had opened at the London Hippodrome, *Round in Fifty*, and other filmmakers added to the tradition in the wake of the Todd adaptation. In "Foggbound," a 1960 episode of the CBS western series *Have Gun—Will Travel*, series hero Paladin, who regularly encounters real and fictional characters of his time in the old west, assists Verne's hero on the American leg of his journey. Less credibly, another descendant of Fogg is assisted by a tripartite Passepartout in the form of *The Three Stooges Go Around the World in a Daze* (1963). Offerings would also use animation, such as *Around the World in 79 Days*, an irregular prestige item on the 1969-71 ABC series, *Cattanooga Cats*.

Despite the many options taken in presenting Verne's novel to viewers, only once—and possibly twice—has the stage play of Verne and d'Ennery been on the screen. The first version was likely the German production, *Die Reise um Die Erde in 80 Tagen*, released March 20, 1919, a silent film apparently lost today. Although universally credited in press notices as based on the novel, it includes two characters only found in the play, Nemea (Kate Oswald) and Archibald Corsican

Corsican and Fogg at right in the 1919 movie.

(Reinhold Schunzel). A mention of shipwreck and attempted suicide in *Vossische Zeitung*, and reference in a review from *Berliner Zeitung am Mittag* to the Eccentric's Club of the Verne/d'Ennery play, rather than the Reform Club of the novel, seems to clinch the case for the source in the play. Moreover, some other articles quoting characters use lines coming directly from the play and not from the novel. The Verne/d'Ennery play had been a great success in Austria and Germany (playing in Berlin, Munich, Braunschweig, Göttingen, and Frankfurt), and had been published several times in more or less faithful adaptations, from 1885 to the 1920s.[1]

Richard Oswald, producer-writer-director of *Die Reise um Die Erde in 80 Tagen*, may have utilized aspects of the play to be sure to have a role for his wife, who played Nemea. Others in the cast included Anita Berber as Aouda, Eugen Rex as Passepartout, Max Gulstoff as Fix, Paul Morgan as John Forster, and Conrad Veidt starring as Fogg. Oswald was acclaimed for capturing all the humor and action of Verne's work in his two-hour movie (long for the time), in eight acts. Despite having a modest budget, it was noted as much superior to the 1913 version

---

1. Volker Dehs, email to Brian Taves, May 10, 2011.

(which was, however, curiously labeled by critics as a French film).[2] *Die Reise um Die Erde in 80 Tagen* seems to have been released in shortened form in the United States as *Around the World in 80 Days* in 1921 by Kinema Film Service for churches, schools, and community centers.

The only overt filming of the play was a 1975 French television program in two parts running a total of three hours. Sadly, *Le Tour du monde en quatre-vingts jours* was an overstated hodgepodge marred by poor casting. Phileas Fogg is played by Jean Le Poulain, a balding comedy singer who appears much older than his 51 years, with only a monocle to assert his British nationality. He radiates neither romance nor heroism, and his casting makes the actions of the character unbelievable. Pierre Trabaud as Passepartout is equally advanced in years, his hair in a combover and proving consistently susceptible to Fix's unconvincing disguises—even Fix as a dance-hall hostess in San Francisco. Aouda is in her mid thirties, but is even less redolent of India than Fogg is of England, nor is the much younger Nemea, played by Yannick Le Poulain.

Archibald (Maurice Rich) is full of bluster and quarrelsome, forcing several duels with Fogg and bested in each. He is impossible to believe as a partner for Nemea; indeed, the romance is handled in the most perfunctory manner. Only Fix (Roger Carrol), foolish but winking at the audience in his various disguises, is appropriate.

Throughout, songs and dances have been added in a musical comedy style, but reflecting none of the Verne/d'Ennery spectacle. The musical numbers are excessive in quantity, often clashing with the narrative, resulting in more noise than cohesion. The opening credits of a circling globe surrounded by dancers following their own circle, wearing costumes of different nations, is sadly the high point of creativity.

Shot on video, the colors are bright and varied, but the sets vary, sometimes creative and stylized, while other times wholly unconvincing, and in a few cases strictly realistic, resulting in an unharmonious clash. Periodically the characters are added with backgrounds shot later, resulting in a limning around the performers, especially when a puff of smoke changes color and reveals the awkwardness of the process.

No less than the style, the adaptation of the playscript makes various inflections and shifts in emphasis. Beginning at the London

---

2. My thanks to John Soister for sharing his research on the film for his book, *Conrad Veidt on Screen* (Jefferson, NC: McFarland, 2009).

Fogg imperiled in the 1975 mini-series starring Jean Le Poulain.

Eccentric's Club in 1872, Phileas Fogg is a heavy-handed president who punctuates the completion of business with the tooting of a horn. The members are seated around a conference table, the Union Jack as table cloth to suggest nationality, but with the club represented in an entirely realistic manner. To the audience, Passepartout reveals his master passes from chair to fireplace in the same number of steps each day. Similarly, the play had used frequent asides, especially by Passepartout, and almost as often by Fix. Fogg hires Passepartout from the club for his manservant, but there seems no distinction between their nationalities. The wager itself becomes merely an extension of Fogg's dictatorial manner, his belief in his own infallibility.

Shifting to Egypt, Fix of the international police tries to create trouble for Fogg, and begins an intermittent collaboration with Archibald. The set of the Egyptian docks itself is realistic, despite obviously flat backgrounds, with beggars stealing from passengers and the local women dancing to satisfy Passepartout's curiosity. By contrast, India is little more than hanging vines. Fix finally reveals his true identity to Passepartout, but for the moment all must cooperate in the rescue. The priest and his yellow-clad servants prepare Aouda for the temple pyre, but as the fire is about to be lit, the old rajah comes to life—Fogg in disguise. (This, of course, is a change from both novel and play, but one designed to make Aouda's gratitude to Fogg more understandable, since the master-servant relationship and her appreciation to Fogg, rather than Passepartout who actually saved her, would be inexplicable for modern audiences unaccustomed to the class system.) The stunned Indians take several moments to realize what has happened, allowing an escape. A fake elephant, who dances as he runs in rhythm with his mahout's dance, takes all into the safety of British territory.

Fogg admires the flowers with a magnifying glass, singing a plaintive love song that leads his bored companions to shush him. Fix is hiding once more while Fogg, in a turban, and Aouda, in English clothes, bridge the divide of their nationalities and dance to reveal their affection. Aouda's ex-servant Nemea asks for their protection and Fogg grants it; Archibald is instantly smitten. (There is a switch in names between Nakahira, Aouda's servant, and Nemea, her sister, between the film and play.) Passepartout, finding Fix, realizes his treachery, but the whole sequence (as in the original play itself) seems rather ponderous, a contrast with other settings that serve to advance the geographical trajectory of the journey.

In the serpent's cavern, the snake goddess, with a Medusa-like hairpiece, leads her maidens in dance. When Fogg and his party take refuge in the cave, they soon find it crawling with the murderous creatures emerging from holes in the rocks. Despite obviously little more than poor puppets, an eerie effect is created. Fogg grabs a bamboo, punches holes in it, converting it into a musical instrument to lure the serpent from imperiling Aouda; Passepartout must tie up and tear apart the snakes that endanger him. Confronting the serpent goddess, only when joined by the spirits of the woods all are saved. (Like the 1919 silent, the 1975 film of the play eliminates the character of Nakahira.)

In part two (beginning with act 3 of the play), Fix, cross-dressing as a dancer, seduces Passepartout into drinking a drug. Fortunately, Archibald comes to the rescue. This introduction of Fix in drag is wholly at variance with the play and serves to diminish the underlying purpose of the scene: a parallel of the "otherness" of the Far East with that of America's west coast. The American West is presented minimally with canvas backdrops, a painted sun, toy train, even an effeminate Indian chief's son with wire frame glasses, forced whimsy combined with menace as two cowboys are mercilessly scalped. The battle with the Indians and the train is almost surreal, and Fogg now goes in advance of the cavalry; Passepartout and Fix are already hiding in Indian costume. Aouda and Nemea are about to be burned at the stake, facing a similar fate as they would have in India. The cavalry engage the Indians in a battle dance, sabre against tomahawk, to banjo music.

On board the *Henrietta*, Passepartout discovers Fix, who had been dressed as a Chinese on the train but is finally in the blackface which had been his disguise in the play since his presentation as a train porter. After buying the boat, Fogg explodes the boiler in an effort to build up more steam—which sends him flying into the air. Nothing but a floating remnant of the deck remains for a refuge. The minimalist backgrounds of the voyage unfortunately remind the viewer of more satisfying cinematic treatments.

At last, home, Fogg is nearly suicidal at his apparent failure. Just as Passepartout, Archibald, Aouda, and Nemea bring news that there is still time, Fix enters with the police. In a scene wholly invented for the film, Fogg wonders if he is dreaming that Aouda had come to him, but he finds her hatpin left behind. With it, he escapes, joining his friends at the Eccentric's Club as the hour strikes. A general celebration breaks out that even Fix is powerless to stop.

This is hardly a faithful adaptation of the play, or the novel, even looking beyond the loss of characterization, and its distortion in the case of Fogg and Archibald. Excised completely is the development of Passepartout's romance with Margaret. Archibald's final heroism in taking the blame for the bank robbery to provide Fogg with the necessary minutes to win his wager is deleted. This loses the theme of Archibald's conversion, with travel affecting his own character as well as Fogg. The experience of the journey impacted both men in a similar manner.

Absent, too, in the simplicity of production design is the spectacle of the original, as epitomized on screen by the facetious treatment of the elephant, eliminating such amusing scenes as the bidding for the pachyderm's service. Admittedly, budget dictates scale, and yet a credible presentation demands a consistency in design, and the conflict between the exactitude, for instance, of the representation of the Eccentric's Club, and the abstraction of the jungles, undermines the work.

Hopefully, future filmmakers, becoming aware of both the play and the novel, may find means to utilize at least some portions unique to the Verne/d'Ennery version in the ongoing effort to render fresh adaptations of *Around the World in Eighty Days*. There are certainly sufficient variations in the play to intrigue audiences, and utilizing precedents actually found in Verne, such as the desire for an additional romance (which played a key role in the 1989 American mini-series) would certainly have been less awkwardly handled with a greater knowledge of the author and the variations he developed to adjust his novel to another medium.

Illustrations

One of the challenges in the Palik series is selecting illustrations, derived from the first French publication of Verne stories in the 19th century and the beginning of the 20th century. Most are either from the stories with which they appeared, or are from other Verne stories, choosing images to match the new context. In this volume, outside of the critical material, the engravings are from the text of the play, *Around the World in 80 Days,* in the original French publication by Hetzel in 1881.

The North American Jules Verne Society is particularly indebted to Bernhard Krauth, chairman of the German Jules-Verne-Club since 2005, for providing the illustrations from Verne stories. A deep sea licensed master working today as a docking pilot in Bremerhaven, Germany, Bernhard has published several Verne-related articles in France, the Netherlands and Germany. Intensely interested in the illustrations of the original French editions of Verne's work, he has been deeply involved in a project to digitize the illustrations, more than 5,000 in all. The project is for common, non-commercial use, and most of the illustrations in this publication were made possible through his generosity.

Acknowledgements

The Palik series, spearheaded by the North American Jules Verne Society, represents a cooperative effort among Vernians worldwide, pooling the resources and knowledge of the various organizations in different countries. The Society is grateful for research assistance to Frédéric Jaccaud, curator of Jean-Michel Margot's Verne Collection at the Maison d'Ailleurs (House of Elsewhere) in Yverdon-les-Bains, Switzerland. The City of Nantes (France), whose Municipal Library has placed all Jules Verne manuscripts online, helped make this publication possible, and the Society would like to thank the City of Nantes and its Bibliothèque municipale (director: Agnès Marcetteau) for their ongoing assistance.

Internationally renowned Verne expert Volker Dehs provided additional details about the early French censorship, initial publication, and German presentations.

The investigations of Stephen Michaluk, Jr., for *The Jules Verne Encyclopedia* (Scarecrow, 1996) into the British and American theatrical presentations, combining evidence from many libraries and archives with copyright registrations, revealed the existence of this translation and extant copy of the play.

John Soister generously shared his research on the 1919 film of the play, some of which had been used in his book, *Conrad Veidt on Screen* (McFarland, 2009).

The Society appreciates the efforts of members who have contributed to this volume, including Kieran O'Driscoll, Jan Rychlík, Noel Gibilaro, and such friends as Elvira Berkowitsch, Jean Frodsham, Pachara Yongvongpaibul, and David March of the Rafael Sabatini website.

Contributors

Philippe Burgaud is a chemical engineer who graduated from the École Nationale Supérieure de Chimie de Paris (ENSCP). He also holds a Ph.D. in Physics and a Master's degree in Economic Science. He has been interested in Jules Verne for decades, and has written numerous articles on Verne related novels, plays and films. His publications have appeared in the *Bulletin de Société Jules Verne*, the *Revue Jules Verne*, in *Historia*, and also in *Téléphonoscope—Revue des amis d'Albert Robida* (*Téléphonoscope—Bulletin of the Friends of Albert Robida*). Burgaud is a member of the Centre International Jules Verne in Amiens.

Jean-Michel Margot is an internationally recognized specialist on Jules Verne. He currently serves as president of the North American Jules Verne Society and has published several books and many articles on the author. Margot edited Verne's theatrical play *Journey Through the Impossible* (Prometheus, 2003) for the Society; a volume of 19th century Verne criticism, titled *Jules Verne en son temps* (Encrage, 2004); and provided the introduction and notes of Verne's *The Kip Brothers* (Wesleyan University Press, 2007).

Brian Taves (Ph.D., University of Southern California) has been an archivist in the Motion Picture, Broadcasting, and Recorded Sound Division of the Library of Congress since 1990. He is the author of over 100 articles and 25 chapters in anthologies, and books on P.G. Wodehouse and Hollywood; director Robert Florey; the genre of historical adventure movies; and fantasy-adventure writer Talbot Mundy, in addition to editing an original anthology of Mundy's best stories. In 2002-2003, Taves was chosen as Kluge Staff Fellow at the Library to write the first book on silent film pioneer Thomas Ince, published by the University Press of Kentucky in 2011. Taves's writing on Verne has been translated into French, German, and Spanish, and he is currently writing a book on the 300 film and television adaptations of Verne worldwide. Taves is coauthor of *The Jules Verne Encyclopedia* (Scarecrow, 1996), and edited the first English-language publication of Verne's *Adventures of the Rat Family* (Oxford, 1993).

JEAN-LOUIS TRUDEL is a science fiction writer, scholar, and translator currently based in Quebec City, Canada. Since 1994, he has authored two novels, two short fiction collections, and twenty-four books for young readers. In collaboration with Yves Meynard, he is also the author of one further novel, one short fiction collection, and three young adult books. He has also written a number of short stories, mostly in French, but also occasionally in English. The holder of degrees in physics, astronomy, and the history of science and technology, he teaches part-time at the University of Ottawa. He has explored the history of science fiction, especially in French-speaking Canada, in a growing number of papers.

The Palik Series

The last two decades have brought astonishing progress in the study of Jules Verne, with new translations of Verne stories, including the discovery of many texts. Still, there remain a number of Verne stories that have been overlooked, and it is this gap that the North American Jules Verne Society seeks to fill in the Palik series.

The North American Jules Verne Society (NAJVS) was formed in 1993, and a decade later, underwrote *Journey Through the Impossible*, the first complete edition in any language of Verne's 1882 science fiction theatrical spectacle, *Voyage à travers l'impossible*. With this experience, and thanks to the generosity of the Society's late member, Edward Palik, a series was commenced to bring to the Anglophone public a series of hitherto unknown Verne tales.

Ed Palik had a special enthusiasm for bringing neglected Verne stories to English-speaking readers, and this will be reflected in the series that bears his name. In this way the Society hopes to fulfill the goal that Ed's consideration has made possible, along with the assistance of a variety of Verne translators and scholars from around the world. The volumes in the Palik series will reveal the amazing range of Verne's storytelling, in genres that may surprise those who only know his most famous stories. We hope to allow a better appreciation of the famous writer who has, for more than a century and a half, been the widest-read author of fiction in the world.

Previous Volumes

The Marriage of a Marquis

Jules Verne is the acclaimed author of such pioneering science fiction as *20,000 Leagues Under the Sea* and *Journey to the Center of the Earth*. Yet he also wrote much more, including stories never before translated into English, which will be presented for the first time in the Palik series, under the auspices of the North American Jules Verne Society.

Foreshadowing such classics as *Around the World in 80 Days*, this inaugural volume focuses on two of Verne's earliest humorous stories, *The Marriage of Mr. Anselme des Tilleuls* and *Jédédias Jamet, or The Tale of an Inheritance*. Translation is provided by Edward Baxter and Kieran O'Driscoll, two of the leading Verne experts; critical commentary examines both stories, and scholars explore why some of the author's stories were overlooked for so many years.

Shipwrecked Family: Marooned with Uncle Robinson

Castaway by pirates on a deserted island… without tools or supplies to survive… a mother and her children have only a kindly old sailor to help. But what explains the strange flora and fauna they find?

The second volume in the Palik series, presented by the North American Jules Verne Society, offers another story never before published in English. *Shipwrecked Family* was rejected by Verne's publisher, so rather than finish it, he began to rewrite it with new characters—and that became the classic, *The Mysterious Island*, where Captain Nemo made his last appearance. Here, then, is Verne's first draft of that novel, one which is very different from the book that it became.

Translation is provided by Sidney Kravitz, also translator of the definitive modern edition of *The Mysterious Island* (Wesleyan University Press, 2002).

Mr. Chimp and Other Plays
Long before Verne stories had formed the basis for such movies as *Around the World in 80 Days*, many of his plays were theatrical blockbusters on the 19th century stage, including several from his novels. Even as he became a novelist, the stage remained crucial to Verne. In this volume, expert scholarly research introduces four of Verne's plays written in his youth, translated by Frank Morlock. Included are *The Knights of the Daffodil*, *Mr. Chimpanzee*, *An Adoptive Son*, and *Eleven Days of Siege*. Verne's themes range from romantic comedies to a scientist's discovery that there may not be such a difference between human and ape after all!

The Count of Chanteleine: A Tale of the French Revolution
This adventure is for everyone who has thrilled to *The Scarlet Pimpernel*, *A Tale of Two Cities*, or *Scaramouche*. A nobleman, the Count of Chanteleine, leads a rebellion against the revolutionary French government. While he fights for the monarchy and the church, his home is destroyed and his wife murdered by the mob. Now he must save his daughter from the guillotine. This exciting swashbuckler is also a meticulous historical re-creation of a particularly bloody episode in the Reign of Terror.

The Count of Chanteleine is the first English translation of this Jules Verne novel, the fourth volume in the Palik series published under the auspices of the North American Jules Verne Society. Commentary by an international team of experts supports the translation by Edward Baxter.

Vice, Redemption and the Distant Colony
Literary fraud or filial devotion? This is the question at the heart of a firestorm that erupted two decades ago. Manuscripts and letters were discovered that proved that Jules Verne's son, Michel, significantly revised over a dozen of the stories published under his father's name, and even originated some of them himself. It was a collaboration that had begun while both were still alive, and continued as Michel saw to posthumous publication many of his father's stories.

In this volume can be found one story as it was written by Jules (as *Pierre-Jean*), and revised by his son (into *The Somber Fate of Jean Morenas*). Michel subsequently brought another version of the same story to the silent movie screen. Also in these pages is the first English translation of a novel Jules began, *Fact-Finding Mission*, but which his son finished, and has hitherto only been available in the completed version by Michel.

The English rendering and notes are by a leading authority on Verne translations, Kieran O'Driscoll.

Additional volumes are underway.

IN 2003, the North American Jules Verne Society also co-published (with Prometheus) a Verne play, *Journey Through the Impossible.*

Jules Verne, the most translated novelist in the world, was also a prolific playwright. *Journey Through the Impossible*, a play of fantasy and science fiction, ran for 97 performances in Paris in 1882 and 1883. In three acts, the characters go first to the center of the Earth, then under the sea, and finally into outer space to the planet Altor. Characters from *Journey to the Center of the Earth, From the Earth to the Moon, Twenty Thousand Leagues under the Sea,* and *A Fancy of Doctor Ox* appear again in *Journey through the Impossible.* The players include Captain Nemo, President Barbicane of the Baltimore Gun Club, Michel Ardan, Doctor Ox, and Professor Lidenbrock. Translation of *Journey Through the Impossible* is by Edward Baxter, with introduction and notes by Jean-Michel Margot, along with reviews from the play's first presentation. Roger Leyonmark provides new illustrations in the style of the 19th century woodcuts that first illustrated French editions of Verne works, and the original engravings from the play are also featured. This is the first complete edition and English translation of a surprising work, by the popular French novelist whose works continue to delight readers—and audiences—to this day.

www.ingramcontent.com/pod-product-compliance
Lightning Source LLC
Chambersburg PA
CBHW051931160426
43198CB00012B/2106